Introduction

Dear Parents,

After 9 years of publishing *PRACTICAL PARENTING NEWSLETTER,* it ceased publication in November-December of 1987.

The wonderful information you, the parents, have shared with me over the years has been passed on to other parents in parts of some of my Practical Parenting books-but not all of it by any means. Your wisdom and good ideas need to be heard by each generation of new parents. That is why we have put together this collection—to keep the information in the hands of those who can profit from it.

I hope you will enjoy reading it as much as I have enjoyed putting it together for you.

Sincerely,

Vicki Lansky

Families

By Jane Howard

Call it a clan, call it a network, call it a tribe, call it a family. Whatever you call it, whoever you are, you need one. You need one because you are human. You didn't come from nowhere. Before you, around you, and presumably after you, too, there are others. Some of these others—in my view about nine, for reasons to be looked at presently—must matter. They must matter a lot to you and if you are very lucky to one another. Their welfare must be nearly as important to you as your own. Even if you live alone, even if your solitude is elected and ebullient, you still cannot do without a clan or a tribe.

But where are you to find one?

What a question. For most of human history, looking for a tribe was the least of anyone's worries. Our tribes and clans were right there in plain sight, like our kneecaps. We were born into tribes, or married into them, or they enslaved us, and that was that. Our tribe kept the howling wolves at bay, and shielded us from savage aliens. It made our decisions for us. It named us, bred us, fed us, taught us how to earn a living, found us our mates, and willed us its property. It told us who we were, what we stood for, and what we might hope to become.

After we died, it honored our memory. It kept us much too busy ever to question its rituals or to wonder whether some other tribe might have been more to our liking.

A couple of anachronistic tribes of this sort still survive today, but most such august and enveloping clans have long since evolved into familes. Families, as all who read newspaper headlines know, are embattled and confused and irksome—so irksome that their members plot and scheme to leave them behind, dwelling at length, the while, on their shortcomings. The United States, as Rebecca West somewhere said, is a nation of middle-aged men running around complaining about their mothers. What folly. What misspent energy. However frail and perforated our families may have become, however they may annoy and retard us, they remain the first of the givens of our lives. The more we try to deny or elude them, the likelier we are to repeat their same mistakes. The first thing we have to do is to stop such efforts. Instead we must come to terms with our families, laughing with them peaceably on occasion if we can manage to, accepting them as the flawed mortals they are, or were, if we cannot.

TABLE OF CONTENTS

THE GUILT ISSUES

THE BETWEEN HUSBAND-AND-WIFE ISSUES

parents forum paren

Q What is the worst discipline

Our son bit when he was mad. We tried everything with no success. He bit a friend one day, and the child's older brother said, "If you do that again, I'll break your teeth." End of problem!

Susan Barnett, Waco, TX

The worst discipline problem I have is deciding when and how to discipline a toddler. I keep telling myself: keep a good sense of humor, don't get in a power struggle, and *teach*, don't punish.

Jane Larrabee, Beverly, MA

Our worst problem is Jennifer talking fresh to us ("I'll do it if I want!"). So far we're trying to explain to her *calmly* that there are some things you just don't say.

Lisa Smith, Hurst, TX

Shane has always been fresh and disrespectful to adults. I began to punish (not physically) every time. My consistency has made a big difference, and at 6 he has finally changed in that regard, although he occasionally lapses.

Myra Weaver, Hollywood, FL

BITING! We solved it by explaining over and over again at kid level that teeth are for chewing food and that mouths are also for talking— to get the anger or frustration out. It was a long stage. It's finally over!

Cam Wilsie, Clio, MI

The most frustrating is "sassing back." Usually I remove myself and the sassy kid from the situation (if it's in public) and then use: Plan A (a firm word), Plan B (a firm hand once on the behind, only if Plan A fails), Plan C (punishment—taking away something the child is really looking forward to). I've only had to use Plan C once with each child. They know I mean business.

Marcia Len, Cohoes, NY

According to friends who are parents of teenagers, the problems I encounter with my little ones are *nothing*. Oh boy, I'll have four teens at once!!!!

Jerri Oyama, Northridge, CA

My son (2) kept telling people to "shut up." I think it's terrible and it grates on me to hear him. As hard as it was not to tell him to stop, we just totally ignored it, and after three months he stopped saying it.

Linda Richardson, Phoenix, AZ

MOST PARENTS SPEND THE FIRST YEARS OF THEIR CHILDREN'S LIVES TEACHING THEM TO WALK AND TALK, AND THE REST OF THEIR LIVES TELLING THEM TO SIT DOWN AND BE QUIET.

They're all terrible. Keeping brother and sister from killing each other is probably the worst. My son also likes to spit. He's managed to teach all the other kids in the park. My daughter has terrible eating habits, and on and on . . . . Nothing's solved and I'm going to the funny farm!

L. Chin, West Linn, OR

Whining, tantrums, negativism—in other words, the "terrible twos"—which I assume will be resolved by firmness, patience, humor, and above all, turning 3!

Pat Spiker, Columbus, OH

Squabbling and fights between my sons (3 and 4). Almost disappeared when I stopped getting involved. *Strongly* recommend CHILDREN: THE CHALLENGE by Dr. Rudolf Dreikurs for this and other useful and practical approaches.

Ann Hoffer, McLean, VA

Bedtime! We tried *everything* for two years! He slept on the floor in our room, on the couch, in our bed, etc. Finally, I told him that when he turned 4 he *had* to sleep in his own bed. It worked, and I'm still trying to figure out why!

Marge Korsi, West Allis, WI

The Great Misunderstanding

Very few parents have difficulty feeling or expressing love toward their children, but many have difficulty expressing authority toward them. There is a pervasive tendency among this generation of parents to view love as a positive force, and authority, or discipline, as a negative one. Instead of communicating authority to their children directly, they do so apologetically or they beat around the bush or procrastinate with pleadings, reasoning, threats, and second chances, making all the more inevitable that which they are trying so desperately to avoid—the anger, the guilt, the resentment.

All this is due to the Great Misunderstanding—that love is somehow more valuable to a child's upbringing than discipline. The Great Misunderstanding has so fogged our common

sense that by some strange twist, while withholding love from a child is generally regarded as abusive, withholding discipline is regarded by many as synonymous with love.

In the real world, however, love is no more important to a child's well-being than the consistent presence of authority figures. Love brings meaning to his life, a reason to strive. Authority provides direction for his strivings. These are not opposite poles, but two sides of the same coin.

In the absence of authority, love becomes over-indulgence—a smothering crippler of self-sufficiency. Likewise, without the tempering effect of love, authority becomes tyranny.

—John Rosemond

John Rosemond is a clinical psychologist, syndicated columnist, and author of PARENT POWER! A COMMON-SENSE APPROACH TO RAISING YOUR CHILDREN IN THE EIGHTIES (Pocket Books) and THE MANAGERIAL PARENT, a parent-training seminar. For information, write to him at PO Box 4124, Gastonia, NC 28054.

forum parents forum

problem you've had?

SO MANY PEOPLE THINK THAT THE MOST IMPORTANT THING IN RAISING CHILDREN IS TO MAKE THEM HAPPY. IT'S NOT. IF YOU RAISE YOUR CHILDREN TO BE DEPENDABLE, INDUSTRIOUS, HONEST, AND CONSIDERATE OF OTHERS, THEY WILL MAKE THEMSELVES HAPPY.

Changing Children's Behavior, J. & H. Krumbaltz

A need to scream (violently, often, and anywhere) over major, minor, and undetermined problems. Resolution came from PRACTICAL PARENTING. We tell our daughter that she can *talk* to us and tell us the trouble, and until she is ready to do so, she is firmly led away. We feel we are disciplined ourselves by being consistent with this approach. Maybe that's the key.

Jodi Junge, Bryn Athyn, PA

Every new one seems to be the worst! Many discipline problems seem to be resolved as the children (and probably parents, too) outgrow them. The one we can't seem to get over is the constant teasing, bickering, and physical fighting between our two boys.

Sally Ann Winterle, St. Paul, MN

Our son was taking a swing at me when I didn't let him do what he wanted. This and most other bad habits have been resolved by taking him by the shoulders, putting my face even with his, and saying, "No more!" loudly. Takes about a week, but it works.

Kathy Hickok, Delray Beach, FL

When my son was 2, he was as wild as they come. He'd hit and punch anyone and everyone. People were full of advice: "Maybe his father's not home enough," "Maybe he watches too much TV." I worried constantly. Now he's 6—very quietly polite and doing very well in school. What changed him? I have no idea! I had pictured him in and out of the principal's office once he reached school, but the only time he visited the principal was to receive a "good citizen" award!

Jill Heasley, Fresno, CA

When my son was 4 he was too aggressive with other children. Separating him from his friends seemed to help.

Bobbie Spallina, Oak Lawn, IL

My 3-year-old often disobeys *loudly* in public. Once in the doctor's office he threw a screaming tantrum. It was so bad, I took him home. Once home, I spanked him too hard, screamed at him, then went upstairs and fell apart emotionally. I reached my limit at that point. Now I'm more consistent and expect him to behave rather than misbehave. Read DARE TO DISCIPLINE and THE STRONG-WILLED CHILD.

Janet Dickinson, Gulfport, MS

My boys are now 18 and 20. Is it old age, or is it really possible that the worst problem I can remember is getting them to do their homework?

Joanie Ecker, Foster City, CA

Handling The Angry Child

Handling children's anger can be distressing for parents. One of the major problems in dealing with anger in children is the angry feelings that are often stirred up in us as a result. As children, we were probably never taught how to deal with anger. We were led to believe that anger was bad, and we were often made to feel guilty for expressing anger. Parents must allow children to feel ALL their feelings. Our goal should not be to repress or destroy angry feelings in children, but rather to accept the feelings and to help channel them constructively.

Here are a few ideas to help you deal with your angry child.

● Provide physical outlets and other alternatives. Exercise and movement can help your child work off anger.

● Use closeness and touching. Move physically closer to the child to curb his or her angry impulses. Young children are often calmed just by having an adult nearby.

● Be ready to show affection. Sometimes all that is needed for an angry child to regain control is a sudden hug or other impulsive show of affection.

● Ease tension through humor. Kidding the child out of a temper tantrum or outburst offers the child a chance to "save face." But remember, there's a big difference between this kind of humor and sarcasm or ridicule.

● Help the child understand the cause of his or her anger. We often fail to realize how easily young children can begin to react properly once they understand the cause of their frustration.

DHEW Publication No. (ADM) 79-781 US Government Printing Office

---

TIME-OUT: AN ALTERNATIVE TO SPANKING

In his book, SOLVING YOUR CHILD'S BEHAVIOR PROBLEMS†, Dr. Jeffrey Kelly recommends using time-out (a brief period of isolation) when a child's misbehavior is too extreme to be ignored. It works, says Dr. Kelly, because being alone and removed from all sources of attention for even a short time is unpleasant for children. He offers these guidelines for using time-out effectively.

● Reserve time-out for serious misbehavior such as tantrums, fighting, aggressiveness, or intentional destruction of things.

● Choose a time-out location that is dull and away from family activities, but safe and non-frightening.

● Use time-out *immediately* after misbehavior occurs.

● For children between 3 and 5, make time-out 5 minutes long. For older children, add 1 minute for each year over 5. (Thus, a 6-year-old will spend 6 minutes in time-out.)

● Don't talk to your child while he or she is in time-out.

● When time-out is over, calmly explain to the child why he or she was punished and what behavior will be expected in the future.

● Make an extra effort to reward good behavior after time-out.

● Be consistent in using time-out and in praising appropriate, positive behavior.

†1983: Little, Brown, & Co., $6.95

parents forum parent

Q When and why would you

I try to check out my emotions first. I don't want to react physically to my children out of my own frustration or anger.

Donna Cianciulli   Miami, FL

Sometimes I let them choose if they want to get spanked or stand in a corner, and I'm surprised whenever they choose the spanking. (I guess it's over with more quickly.) We always discuss *why* they got punished and end up with a hug.

Gina Walker   Hickory Hills, IL

If they continually defy a previously set limit, they get spanked. I have a neighbor who believes you should never hit a child, yet she ends up screaming at her kids till they're all nervous wrecks.

Greta Walsh   Minneapolis, MN

We only spank when our children do something to endanger themselves (run in the street, etc.) or if every other method of discipline has failed and our children are totally out of control.

Blythe Lipman   Millville, NJ

I usually give a verbal warning first. Then if they continue, they get a spanking. I didn't start that until my first child was 3. He is now 4, and for punishment he has to go to his room, which is worse than a spanking for him. I didn't believe in spanking but things were getting out of hand. After just a few confrontations, I found I was getting respect again.

Beth McCormick   Hudson, OH

I save spanking for direct defiance — when my son knows the rule, chooses to break it anyway, and then looks me straight in the eye as if to say, "What are you going to do about it?" Spanking is also used for extremes: touching a hot stove or running into the street. Sometimes the time isn't right for reasoning!

Pat Spiker   Columbus, OH

They usually get sent to their bed or chair to think about what they've done. It just doesn't make sense to say stop hitting or we'll hit you! We try other forms of discipline, but spanking does become necessary at times.

Kim Matthews Chite   Ft. Pierce, FL

Ideally I would never spank my child because the lesson is only that it's OK to hit if you are bigger and stronger. Actually, I only spank my children in the least ideal of situations — when my anger is out of control. While I don't think children should be hit at all, I have to agree with Dr. Hiam Ginott that children should *only* be hit in anger.

Unsigned

My theory is that once a child pushes a parent to spank him, even though it's the child who gets hurt, he is still the "winner." I think that if they know they won't get spanked, they also know that they have to take responsibility for their own actions sometime.

Karen Haynes   Upper Marlboro, MD

Keep Your Temper.

Nobody Wants It.

Anger Is Only One Letter

Short of Danger.

Hitting by any other name is still hitting, and in my book it's wrong, period. I don't hit dogs, I don't hit other adults, and I don't hit my child.

Susan Roberts   Jackson, MS

Nicholas is 5 and has been spanked twice: once when he was about to get burned on the stove and didn't listen to get away, and once when he was purposely being nasty. It worked both times and he was very sorry. I'm sure it worked because spanking is not an everyday occurrence. I only resort to it when it's absolutely necessary.

Kris Taranec   Lake Havasu, AZ

I spank when I have reached the breaking point. The kids know I've reached the limits of tolerance and it clears the air. Children need limits, and nothing else says so loudly and clearly "you have gone too far."

Janet Gift   Davis, CA

Only if the child put himself in extreme danger — like the time my 3-year-old grabbed a sharp knife from the dishwasher and ran away with it.

Maryann Shutan   Highland Park, IL

I have three children and I have spanked a total of five times. I can remember each time because I can look back and see that I struck out in anger. I believe that a child cannot learn "internal control" or "discipline" from a spanking. All spanking does is undermine the child's self-esteem and put you in a "one-up" position. I refuse to do that, and my children have flourished because of it.

Nedra O'Neill   Evergreen Park, IL

Usually just being sent to their room for 10-15 minutes works. But I don't believe it's possible to simply reason with children and never spank. I've yet to see anyone successfully reason with a 2-year-old.

Donna Schreier   St. Paul, MN

Never! How can the hands that hug her also cause her pain? Hitting children demonstrates to them that it is OK to hit, and that might makes right.

Donna Whitehill   Champaign, IL

When I was pregnant with my first child, my husband and I discussed this. He said, "We'll never spank this child." After my son was born, I agreed. Instead, I have always guided him lovingly. When he went into the street, I would show him big cars and explain the danger. Later when he could understand more, I explained how frightened I felt that he might get hurt. He cared about my feelings and obeyed. He's always been well-behaved because I calmly explained to him the reasons he couldn't do things. If I couldn't think of a good reason not to, then I let him do what he wanted. I see acquaintances who spank and shout — it doesn't work!

Joanne Schenendorf   Woodbury, NY

Ideally, I don't believe in spanking at all. I try to follow *Your Child's Self-Esteem* (Dorothy C. Briggs, Doubleday), and most of the time it works. However, when it comes to safety, I expect my son to mind.

Vicki Piipo   Richland, WA

forum parents forum

spank your child?

from *Do They Ever Grow Up* by Lynn Johnston

I wish I could say I've never spanked my child, but I have occasionally. I don't think it's right. Spanking proves nothing. It says "you have to do what I want because I'm bigger." Even a swat on the behind is an act of aggression. Fitzhugh Dodsen in *How to Parent* says spanking should never occur except if you're angry. Children can understand anger, but not a detached sort of spanking. Apologize and make up as soon as possible and talk about child and parent behavior.

Unsigned

Like other parents, I try not to spank in anger, but my mother (who raised five of us) said to go with my instincts instead of by the book. And sometimes spanking is a natural reaction.

Denise Voeller   Coon Rapids, MN

I think spanking occurs when parent and child are frazzled or out of control, and it only adds fuel to a potentially explosive situation. As Erma Bombeck says, the child who needs a hug is probably acting his or her worst. Same for moms.

Cam Wilsie   Clio, MI

Both of our children get "popped" on the behind when they are totally outrageous or when they deliberately disobey. But we don't spank in the sense our parents did — in the basement on a bare bottom until it was red, or even with hair brushes or belts.

Kathryn Richardson   Ft. Defiance, AZ

I have spanked my child twice (she's 4). Both times I was out of control and I felt terrible afterwards. I felt *small* and inferior. Why couldn't I think of a better way to handle the situation? I think spanking shows your child that hitting is a way to solve a problem. I don't want my child to learn that.

Francie Gass   Bellingham, WA

Our family rule is that you get spanked if you step into the street. We have always lived in places where this was much too dangerous for discussions.

Sharon Amastae   El Paso, TX

I hate spanking my child. I hated being spanked as a child. I remember it most as a teenager, and it was very degrading. My husband and I do it mostly to show we mean business when repeated warnings are not heeded.

It's never more than a swat on the (fully clothed) bottom. Since reading *How To Talk So Kids Will Listen and Listen So Kids Will Talk* by Faber & Mazlish (Rawson, Wade), I expect never to need to spank again.

Marie-Anne Scarpelli   Ontario

I have spanked my daughter (2-1/2) about five times, each time with an explanation beforehand. Afterwards I always felt like I had accomplished nothing but to shock and hurt her. I plan on never doing it again.

Susan Keck   Gaithersburg, MD

WE spank as soon as they defy us, even if it means going into the washroom of a restaurant or leaving church for a few minutes. Many "experts" say not to spank a child when you're angry, but to me that's the most natural thing to do, and the best time to get the point across. A small child has a short memory and if you wait until you get home, they will not associate their behavior with the punishment.

Kathy S.   Burbank, IL

I think that outright disobediance, defiance, or disrespect most certainly call for a spanking. Remember: spare the rod and spoil the child.

Jeanne Fedoryshyn   Palm Harbor, FL

The Balance of Power

Parents puzzle a great deal about discipline these days. Many parents lean too much in one direction or the other.

I see some parents who are much too easy on their children. These parents hardly ever say "No" and hardly ever make their "No" stick. Sometimes these parents act this way because they don't want to make their youngster unhappy. Other such parents may be a little lazy. They don't want to work at discipline, and they don't follow through.

To a youngster wise rules and regulations actually mean love. They mean: Someone is watching out for me, someone cares. Wise rules and regulations mean safety. The youngster knows deep down: I'm not old enough yet to run the ship. It is very frightening to a child to feel that parents have given up and that the child is in charge.

Have some standards and expectations, but don't hesitate to make an exception now and again. And don't hesitate to change any rule that simply leads you into one hassle after another. You can be firm and strict and still use you heart and use your head. And you can be firm and strict without using a heavy hand and a harsh tongue. Being firm doesn't mean to hurt. Being firm means that you have confidence to help and teach your child.

Some parents need to relax a bit. To give the child more elbow room. Just as other parents need to buck up and to tighten up. It is not easy to get the right mixture; it is hard to strike a balance. Yet the path to good discipline lies in finding the right mixture.

James L. Hymes, Jr. author and educator

If it is a situation in which they have previously learned right from wrong, but are headed toward the wrong, we count to three to give them a chance to correct themselves. If they don't, we spank them and explain why. Counting gives them a chance to think.

Janet Hare   Omaha, NE

Only when I've lost control! Ninety-eight percent of the spankings I've given my child occurred after my second child was born because I was so tired. Normally I use natural and logical consequences (following Dreikurs and P.E.T.). To hit a child is sinful to me.

Michele McBrayer   Georgetown, KY

parents forum paren

Q How do you build your child's

On each child's birthday I present him/her with a book of pictures from the preceding year, showing his/her growth and development with a little rhyme under each picture. My kids love their birthday books and want to hear me read them over and over.

Janet Gift Davis, CA

We play a game in the car, in the bathtub, in the kitchen, or wherever. I say, "Danny, you are TEEEERIFIC!" and he says back, "I am TEEEERIFIC!!" We do it till we have to stop for some reason, usually giggle fits!

Marcia Len Cohoes, NY

I consciously and consistently think to comment on what our children have accomplished or done right *daily*: "You did your zipper all by yourself without getting frustrated!" "I liked the way you shared with Jason when he was over today." Any little compliment helps.

Jodi Junge Bryn Athyn, PA

I think the positive approach of a Montessori education has made a big difference in our children's self-esteem. I think children blossom in an environment in which they are genuinely loved (and are told so!), in which they are accepted as capable human beings, and in which there is loving guidance provided.

Mary Ellen Cooper Glendale, AZ

I "wow" and "that's great" and "I'm so proud of you" them to death.

Maureen Deitsch Toledo, OH

We sing a lot about her, using her name in the songs.

Joy Goldwasser Denver, CO

When my daughter comes home from school and tells me one of her friends can do something better, I always try to show her different things that she does well.

Blythe Lipman S. Windham, ME

I have an "art gallery" along one wall of a long hallway where I frame and hang the artwork my 3-year-old brings home from preschool.

Amy Trestman New Orleans, LA

I love and accept her for who she is and point out the positive. I kiss her and tell her I love her LOTS!

Kris Gialdini Fremont, CA

My mother was fond of labels: "You're stupid," "you clumsy idiot," etc., so I'm careful not to do the same thing.

Pat Spiker Columbus, OH

When I'm teaching Sean, I never say "no" when correcting his reaction. If I ask which is the blue balloon and he points to the red one, I say "That's the red one," and either ask again or point the blue one out. When learning something new, a child doesn't need to be told he's wrong.

Jennifer Norman Glen Ellyn, IL

I try to listen to my daughter (3) when she wants to tell me something; it's always so. important! We try never to make fun of her when she's playing or attempting something new. We let her work at something alone until she does it or asks for help. We commend her on things done well (by her standards, not ours).

Betsy Jacquez Cincinnati, OH

Respect

Respect is something valued by all
Whether we're big or whether we're small.
Grown-ups, at times, seem to forget
That even though children aren't grown-up yet,
They deserve to be treated in the very same way
When it comes to their feelings or what they say.
To a friend or a peer, I have little doubt,
That most adults would refrain from shouting out,
"Sit up straight at the table and eat all on your plate!"
Or, "I'm busy right now. You'll just have to wait."
"Look how sloppy you are! Can't you ever stay
    clean?"
"That's the messiest room I've ever seen!"
Children need love and to be helped to grow.
And one way to do this is to let them know
You respect their right to do it their way.
And you'll listen—really listen—to what they say.
Respect from adults builds self-respect in a child.
It tells them their thoughts and feelings are valued
    and worthwhile.
So take some time to reflect, to think for a while:
Do you give your friends more respect
Than you do your child?
Nancy Hopkins

We sing the Sesame Street song "Keep on trying and trying again." We give lots of hugs and tell her how glad we are that she's our daughter.

Karen Dockrey Burke, VA

We have always treated our children with respect. We listen to them, have them contribute to family decisions, and really make them feel that their opinions and feelings count (because they do). We also don't interrupt them. We admit that no one is perfect, including parents, and that we all make mistakes.

Unsigned

Compliments go a long way, especially when they overhear you telling your spouse or another adult about something they did or said.

Cynthia Wagner Montebello, CA

After watching Lindley for 9½ months, I'm convinced that he was born with self-esteem and I merely try not to take it away. I provide SOS—security, opportunity, and safety.

Sarah Schiermeyer Weston, MA

My son is only 2, but I let him make some of his own decisions such as what to wear and which TV show to watch, within the choices I'll allow.

Janet Bauer Islip Terrace, NY

We have started traditions to help our children realize their important place in the family. We enjoy celebrating birthdays especially. This spring when our little girl turns 3, we will show pictures and slides of her birth and of her first and second birthdays. We did this last year and she was so happy she cried tears of joy.

Cheryl Sedlmeyer Ft. Wayne, IN

When my son started to read we made a big poster for his room that says "Andrew is a good boy!" He loves to read it over and over to us.

G. Pappas Dudley, MA

I recommend two great books: HIDE OR SEEK by James Dobson and PARENTHOOD WITHOUT HASSLES—WELL, ALMOST by Kevin Leman. Both authors recommend saying "good job, well done" etc. instead of "good boy" or "good girl." This puts the emphasis on the act (good or bad) rather than on the child. I catch myself doing it the other way all the time.

Cynthia Carlton Los Angeles, CA

forum parents forum

self-esteem?

I watch and listen to Mister Rogers and try to do as he does. I tell my daughter, "You are special."

Francie Gass Bellingham, WA

I never ask "What's that?" about his artwork. Instead I ask him to tell me a story about it.

Eileen Schanelklitsch Havertown, PA

We let our children see their grandparents as much as possible. Grandparents are the best builders of a child's self-esteem.

Ellyn Wiechert O'Fallon, IL

I worry about this because I have trouble with my own self-esteem and so does their father. I make sure I show them *often* how much I love them. I speak to them as I would to a friend (because I really *like* them).

Kathy Hickok Delray Beach, FL

We praise Chris when he tries to do something new or does something well. Mistakes are OK. I've heard some women call their children stupid and dumb when they don't do something correctly.

Linda Newberry Jermyn, PA

I always tell Jamie (3) what a lucky day it was for Mommy and Daddy when he was born.

Linda Richardson Phoenix, AZ

Every night at bedtime I tell my son how much Daddy and I love him. I also tell him that he is a good person and we will always like and love him. Sometimes he does things we don't like, but we always like *him*.

Mona Hanlin Hartland, WI

Touching and eye contact are very important. I try to get down at the same level as my children and look them in the eye when we talk. I also think lots of hugs are important. Both of these things tell them they're important and special.

Karen Bowen Sandwich, IL

I try to always *listen* to my kids and make them feel that what they have to say is just as important as what adults say. I used to hate it when I was a kid and people treated me as an inferior.

Jeanne Gretter Sigourney, IA

I tell my sons regularly how much I like being with them, because I do! They are great people and they make me laugh.

Nancy Wrather Los Angeles, CA

Give your child a

WARM FUZZY

I allow my son to do things for himself as much as possible. The look of joy and pride when he claps his hands and says, "I did it all by myself" tells me I'm doing the right thing.

Colette Seieroe San Jose, CA

I try to acknowledge all of my son's feelings. He knows that anger and frustration are just as okay as the good feelings, and that learning to express them in acceptable ways helps to make them go away. I accept his angry tirades and we talk about them. I think this helps him to be more demonstrative with his good feelings, too. He's quick with a hug and an "I love you." I think he will be very comfortable with his emotions and feelings about himself later because he knows that he's not "bad" for feeling a negative emotion.

Susan Skolnick Sunland, CA

I have tried to make a definite statement that love and affection are not rewards, but are for the most part unconditional. Q.: "Why does Daddy love you?" A.: "Just because I'm ME!"

Tom Brink Grand Rapids, MI

My husband grew up in a family where equality was stressed. The two boys often received identical toys or one to share. He was the younger and always felt he got what his big brother wanted. So we try to give gifts that fit each child's personality and preferences.

Becky Wilkins Lubbock, TX

Motivational charts with stickers have helped my 5-year-old. He sees the progress he's making towards a particular goal. The mistakes are downplayed. Taking him out by himself to a show, for a meal, or shopping seems to make him feel more secure, loved, and worthy of love.

Becky Gammons Beaverton, OR

We use definite statements about actions: "You jumped high." "You brushed your teeth before you were told." This is recommended in BETWEEN PARENT AND CHILD by Dr. Haim Ginott.

K. Darnell Hueytown, AL

Self-Esteem: What Does It Mean?

Self-esteem is significant in every aspect of life. How we act, how we learn, how we relate to others, and how we work are all determined by our beliefs and attitudes about ourselves.

Self-esteem is a personal assessment of worthiness. It indicates the extent to which we believe ourselves to be capable, significant, successful, and worthy.

Persons with high self-esteem appear poised and confident. Their social relationships are generally good. They are less influenced by peers and tend to make better decisions. People with low self-esteem may feel isolated, unloved, and defenseless. They perceive themselves as being powerless to attain what they desire from life.

It is almost impossible to underestimate the impact of self-esteem on a person's life. Study after study has shown that children with superior intelligence but low self-esteem may do poorly in school, while children of average intelligence but high self-esteem can be unusually successful.

How does one achieve high self-esteem? Four basic conditions are necessary (1) *Connectiveness* means that a person gains satisfaction from associations with others and is affirmed by them. (2) *Uniqueness* is a special sense of self that involves respecting one's own individuality and knowing that others do too. (3) A sense of *power* involves feeling we are in charge of our own lives. (4) *Models* help us establish meaningful values, goals, ideals, and standards.

In creating a positive environment for children, parents must not forget to reflect on their own feelings of self-esteem. Studies indicate that high parental self-esteem is one of four important factors in the home that influence self-esteem. The others are: total or near total acceptance of the children by their parents, clearly defined and enforced limits, and respect and latitude for individual action within those limits.

In this rapidly changing world, parents are challenged to determine what children need to cope with an unpredictable future. Self-esteem should top the list; it will give them the confidence to seek the best from themselves and from their world.

from "Our Children's Self-Esteem," Network Publications, a division of ETR Associates, 1983, Santa Cruz, CA

At this age (15 months) I find a simple smile and hug whenever he discovers something new and exciting sends him off to show his father or the dogs what he has learned.

Pam Holbrook Pomona, CA

parents forum parent

Q How do you REALLY toilet train a child?

An observation after reading your answers: until the milestone is passed, the question of toilet training is monumental. In retrospect, it seems like no big deal. The trick, it seems, is to relax, let the kids take the lead, make it their responsibility, not yours. And praise. . .praise. . .PRAISE. Many parents have found the three books mentioned here very helpful.

You DON'T. Toileting is a learned, developmental process, not something you train a child to do. Give him the information he needs (wet, dry, removing his own clothes, proper time to sit on potty, positive reinforcement that he can do it himself), and he will learn to do it himself.

Rebecca Kajander, Wayzata, MN

Remain calm; as the child learned to walk, gave up the bottle and ate solid foods, s/he will use the toilet. Don't worry about friends' and relatives' stories about their children being trained at 18 or 24 months — you know your child, and their stories could be exaggerated a bit!

Sharon Schaff, Riverview, MI

Reverse psychology worked like a charm with my third. It was during midterms; she kept ripping her diaper off and I kept putting it back on and wishing we could postpone the whole process. Being a determined child, she persisted, and I submitted, grumbling. She was totally trained in two days.

Cynthia Orloff, Detroit, MI

THREE THINGS YOU CANNOT DO FOR ANYONE ELSE: EAT, SLEEP AND GO TO THE TOILET
Helen Wheeler Smith

Don't do anything except show the child where the bathroom is. When the child is ready — try to stop him/her. You won't be able to!

Deborah Smollen, Middlefield, CT

With lots of love and tons of patience. Seriously, I feel this is an ordeal for every child, and too often we parents label a child's reluctance as laziness, when it is really fear. Think about it — scary, isn't it?

Nedra O'Neill, Calumet Park, IL

Our daughter knew all along what it was about, and that when she was big enough, she would use the potty/toilet, too. We gave her a potty chair when she was 2, and left it up to her. Over a period of two to three weeks, just before she was 3, she trained herself completely. She was proud, and the accident rate has been almost zero. I'm convinced! I've watched several friends try the "traditional" training route and in general, the successes are pretty marginal and the failures frustrating for parents and children.

Katherine Z. Walker, Bradford, VT

We put our son in training pants. He wet his pants and down his leg once, and after that he told me whenever he had to go.

Vivian Hain, Shillington, PA

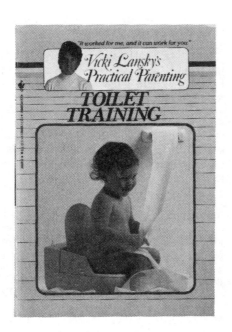

Practical Parenting TOILET TRAINING deals with everything from readiness to bedwetting information.

With our first two children, it wasn't accomplished until after they were 3, using M & Ms for reinforcement. I started on our third, when she was 2, to screams of "I'm stuck, I'm stuck!" I quit. What's the hurry, when I know I probably won't succeed until she's 3 anyway?

Barbara Thode, Wayzata, MN

You don't — you wait for their bodies to mature (a fact God has already worked out). I made a game of it, with a timer set for 15 minutes after a liquid. He loved it.

Linda Hurstell, Vicksburg, MS

These days, potty training takes on a lot of the aspects of a first kiss. You can't *do* much about it; it just happens. Mostly you sit around and wonder when your kid will put together the proper inclination and situation — and presto! he or she is trained. In my case, potty training occurred over a weekend. The key, I found out by accident, was that Molly didn't want to be taken to her potty and prompted (how silly of me to think that *that* would work!) but rather, characteristically, wanted to DO IT HERSELF. Once we got that straight, there was no problem, except to praise the results. And how we did praise her! It got to be a real circus, particularly when she crowed "I go poopie!" (her word, not mine) in the midst of a dinner party. We all called our encouragement toward the bathroom, but that wasn't enough. Proud as punch, out she paraded with her treasures, shuffling around in her pulled-down pants and panties. What luck that our guests are understanding parents themselves — they've been there too.

Kathe Grooms, St. Paul, MN

forum parents forum

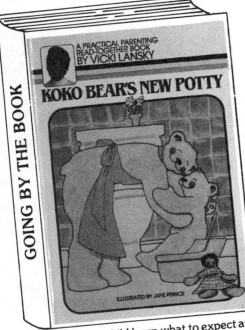

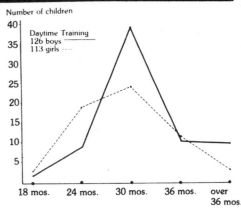

KoKo helps a child learn what to expect and what's expected.

I *really* need help in this area! At age 3, Ryan positively refuses to have BMs on the potty—he insists on a diaper. He is big for his age, and squeezing him into his diaper is hard. He is upset if he does "go" in his pants, but is positively frantic if I suggest he sit on the potty. He was easy to train for urinating—but the BMs are another story. All the books say bowel training comes first, so this was surprising to me. Any other moms with this problem?
Sandra Heath, Brownsville, TX

From the responses we've gotten, I would say you are definitely not alone. —VL

Instead of using a potty seat on the stool, I started my boys out facing the tank. Both can get off and on by themselves, and have done this since they were 1½ years old. When facing backward, they don't see the l-o-n-g way to the floor and don't have a fear of falling. They also have the security of the seat to hang on. Sure is nice not to have to take a seat around!
Paula D. Brooks, Sacramento, CA

I found my son needed a potty chair with arms on it to brace himself when having a bowel movement.
Sally Ann Winterle, St. Paul, MN

Do I train them? I always got the feeling they were training me! The discovery of an allergic problem with one of our children was not in any way aided by our pediatrician. After reading an article in PREVENTION magazine, I pulled her off milk. Joy of joys, she was dry for the first time in years. We're still finding other allergies, but at least now she knows it's a physical problem and not something wrong with her as a person.
Catherine Poulos, Park Ridge, IL

Let them know you think going to the bathroom in the big pot is a neat trick, and don't worry about it. Do you know any teens who use diapers?
Frances Putnam, San Diego, CA

Have a potty chair on each level of the house.
Use loose-fitting undies and pants for ease in pulling up and down.
Rewards? I think *I* deserve a reward for potty training twins. If one of them wasn't running to the bathroom, I was!
Robyn Neuman, Beaver Dam, WI

Other Rewards Used by Parents

Many of you seemed concerned that a reward system, especially one of candy, was too detrimental; others thought not. Here are some of the additional ideas you've come up with:
- Stars or stickers (on a calendar) and success charts
- M & Ms, candy kisses, jelly beans, and peppermints
- Penny gumball machine
- Cheese balls, fish crackers, Life cereal
- Pieces of fruit
- Little wrapped gifts in a glass bowl
- "Big Boy pants"/pretty panties/a shopping trip for new underwear
- Hugs and kisses
- Being pushed on a swing
- Calling Grandma on the phone

Above, the results of the PP survey. It's true — girls are generally trained earlier than boys!

Out of exhaustion and frustration, I gave my daughter chocolate as a reward for daytime training, at about 2½ years. It worked: I was in heaven, and she was proud. That night, I went into her room several times while she was asleep and gently whispered in her ear, asking her not to wet her bed. She woke up dry, ready to use her potty. Gradually I stopped the rewards, but continued the nightly "suggestions," and she was trained, both day and night. After about a week, I stopped the nightly visits, and she wet the bed. I started them again, continued for about a week, and tapered off gradually. Some may dispute the validity of this method, but for me it worked. (Many researchers believe there are periods during sleep in which we are receptive to suggestions and learning.)
Sherry Weinstein, Scotch Pl., NJ

The problem is: how do you RE-TRAIN the child when baby #2 comes along!
Michelle Sheehy, Roseville, MN

Ha! You just keep trying. And trying . . . and trying. Wait for warm weather, after the child is 2 — only shirts and underpants to change makes for less aggravation than long, heavy pants, plus socks and shoes.
Lea Moran, Cortland, OH

I've decided to leave it up to my daughter's (future) husband!
Lyn Souter, Onalaska, WI

parents forum paren

Q What words of condolence have

My children and I lost a very close friend this summer. It was a little girl who went to the school where I teach (she was in my class) and where my children go to school. It was hard on all of us—especially me! I let the kids know how sad I was, and they often saw me crying.

Sometimes they cried right along with me. The most comforting thoughts for her family and those grieving for her were that we would one day all be together again in Heaven. This experience has made my children much less fearful of dying, because they know that now they have a special friend waiting for them in Heaven.

Mary Ellen Cooper, Glendale, AZ

When my beloved mother died, the only words of comfort that really had an effect came from within myself: As long as she is remembered, she is not completely gone. The most distressing comment (which I heard often): "She's better off now." Although she suffered somewhat, this comment really irritated us.

Myra Weaver, Hollywood, FL

When my mother died I was touched by the letters I received from her friends telling me of some fond remembrance each one had of her. Even now, eight years after her death, I want to hear people talk about her.

Pat Brankmann, Palo Alto, CA

Recently my father died, and my brother's boss said, "I hope time passes quickly, as that's what it's going to take to get through this period—time." This was so genuine and sincere, did not attempt to take away our grief, respected our needs to readjust and *include* this loss in our daily living.

Elaine Whitlock, Northampton, MA

No words are necessary; just listen and let the person talk about her pain. Actions speak louder than words. Be there for her, and do whatever needs to be done. Please remember that the grief process is not over in a few weeks but takes months, even years. The initial shock right after the event carries you through the funeral and a few weeks beyond. Often the numbness wears off right around 4-6 weeks, and that's when people stop calling and caring—just when you need them the most.

Judi Welsh, Apple Valley, MN

My daughter (4 at the time) lost a 6-year-old friend from a brain tumor. She went quickly, but during those months we made sure she saw her friend in various stages. We taught her that people *always* need love, but to respect her sensitivities about such things as how she looked.

We did not take our daughter to the funeral, but I now think we should have at least gone to the mortuary. We did visit the grave often, with the reminder that it was just her bones, not her spirit there. The child's family was great at sharing memories; hospice helped a lot.

About 6 months later, we moved and the grieving process began anew. I called Compassionate Friends, and thank heaven for their support!

Three excellent books are: *Remember the Secret*, by Elizabeth Kubler-Ross (Celestial Arts, 231 Adrian Rd., Millbrae, CA 94030; $8.95); *About Handicaps*, by Sara Bonnett Stein (Walker & Co., 720 Fifth Av., New York City, NY 10019; $8.95); and *The Fall of Freddy the Leaf*, by Leo Buscaglia (Holt, Rinehart & Winston, 383 Madison Av., New York City, NY 10017; $7.95).

[Name mislaid, sorry.]

Books on the Loss of a Child

Last year, five books were published on this subject—which indicates how little information was available previously.

Recovering from the Loss of a Child, by K. F. Donnelley (Macmillan Co., 866 Third Av., New York City, NY 10022); $13.50.

When Pregnancy Fails, by S. Borg and J. Lasker (Beacon Press, Boston, MA 02108); $6.95.

After a Loss in Pregnancy, by N. Berezin (Simon and Schuster, 1230 6th Av., New York City, NY 10020); $9.25.

The Other Side of Pregnancy, by S. J. Jimenez (Prentice-Hall, Englewood Cliffs, NJ 07632), $5.95.

The Ultimate Loss: Coping with the Death of a Child, by J. Bordow (Beaufort Books, 9 E. 40th St., New York City, NY 10016); $12.95

My third son died 22 hours after birth from hypoplastic left heart (the left half of his heart was underdeveloped). We knew nothing about the birth defect until shortly before his death. My other two sons (ages 6½ and 2½) saw Brian shortly after his birth and were told of his death when they came home from school.

The words that hurt the *most* were: "At least you have two healthy boys at home." "It was a blessing he didn't live." "At least you didn't bring him home and become attached to him"—as if I hadn't carried him for nine months!

What helped the most: Several hours of *free* babysitting offered by a mother in my babysitting co-op; a hug; crying with me; letting me talk at any hour. Friends who'd had miscarriages would take to me about the "empty" feelings they'd had. One nurse who'd been through my labor and delivery with me requested to help me when she heard that Brian had died. She offered to screen my phone calls and visitors and, when I did have phone calls, sat with me to comfort me afterward.

Ironically, four weeks after my son's death, my husband had a mild heart attack, and this time I didn't hesitate to ask for prayers, meals from friends, and so forth.

A few people remembered my other two children, following Brian's death and their father's heart attack, and would hug them and pay special attention to their needs.

Only one male friend called specifically to talk with my husband following Brian's death. He had lost a newborn child years ago and was able to console my husband as only a man who had also lost a child could do.

Several people have admitted finally that they didn't know what to say to me or how to act, so they just avoided me; that hurt so much.

Sandy Long, Santa Ana, CA

After having had a miscarriage which overwhelmed me, a relative called me to say how sorry she was that I had lost my baby. She was only one of two people who didn't refer to the life inside of me as "just a fetus."

Maryann Shutan, Highland Park, IL

Just listening is the best thing you can offer. Allowing people to ventilate their feelings is better than any words.

Dana Clark, Santa Barbara, CA

forum parents forum

helped you most in dealing with a loss?

After two years of trying to have a baby, I finally learned I was pregnant. Two days later, I miscarried. I was, of course, bitterly disappointed and feeling totally inadequate. Through my grief I confessed to a friend, "I guess I just wasn't meant to have children."

He looked me straight in the eye and said, "Maybe you were meant to adopt."

Suddenly I saw my situation in a whole new light.

That was five years ago. I now have three beautiful daughters (not adopted—so much for my infertility!). I still think of that statement whenever I'm feeling like a failure in any area. It helps to remind myself that there are some things we are meant to do and some we're not, and we all need to recognize our own niches.

Barbara Sattora, Rush, NY

Shortly after the miscarriage of our first child, my husband and I received the following note from my parents:

"Our thoughts and prayers are with you in this time of stress and disappointment. We hope and pray God will give you the strength to accept His will, and that this time of trial will bring you closer to Him and to each other. We love you and wish that we could bear the pain for you, but God in His wisdom does what is best for each of us. When you have recovered from all of this, we hope you will find consolation and hope in your faith in God, and in our love and faith and compassion for you both.

"All our love, Mama and Daddy"

This message of love and support brought tears to our eyes and an overwhelming sense of comfort and hope. My parents, having raised 20 children of their own, truly understand the miracle of birth. We hope their words of support may comfort others who may be dealing with such a loss.

Dee Dee Breal, Ft. Worth, TX

We lost our 10-month-old son, Bradley, to an accident two years ago and now have a 1-year-old son, Scott. Words I remember and live by are these: Our son was not simply "taken" from us. Rather, he was "given" to us for 10 happy months. We feel honored to have been chosen to be his parents, chosen to teach him what we did, an chosen to love him and tuck him in at night. I feel we also have been chosen to help others bear this great tragedy with comforting. *Chris Cooper, Mukilteo, WA*

There are really no words that can help in the event of the death of a loved one. (I know—I just lost my father this year.) But, as the old adage goes, "Action speaks louder than words." Be there for your friend, and offer your help if you really care—clean a room, babysit, or make dinner.

Mrs. Roger Gladstone, Great Neck, NY

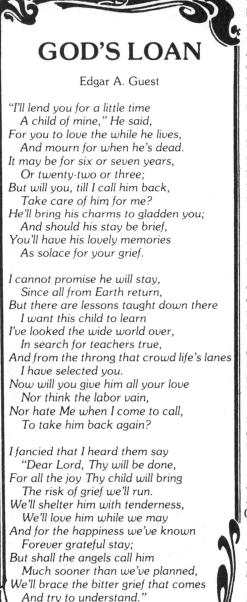

GOD'S LOAN

Edgar A. Guest

*"I'll lend you for a little time
   A child of mine," He said,
For you to love the while he lives,
   And mourn for when he's dead.
It may be for six or seven years,
   Or twenty-two or three;
But will you, till I call him back,
   Take care of him for me?
He'll bring his charms to gladden you;
   And should his stay be brief,
You'll have his lovely memories
   As solace for your grief.*

*I cannot promise he will stay,
   Since all from Earth return,
But there are lessons taught down there
   I want this child to learn
I've looked the wide world over,
   In search for teachers true,
And from the throng that crowd life's lanes
   I have selected you.
Now will you give him all your love
   Nor think the labor vain,
Nor hate Me when I come to call,
   To take him back again?*

*I fancied that I heard them say
   "Dear Lord, Thy will be done,
For all the joy Thy child will bring
   The risk of grief we'll run.
We'll shelter him with tenderness,
   We'll love him while we may
And for the happiness we've known
   Forever grateful stay;
But shall the angels call him
   Much sooner than we've planned,
We'll brace the bitter grief that comes
   And try to understand."*

I was most distressed by nurses who avoided me because I had had a miscarriage. So often we are scared to approach those who have suffered a loss, but after being in those shoes I learned that I most needed people who would talk openly about what happened.

Jane H. Peifer, Middletown, DE

Although my husband, family, and friends were here to help and support me when my baby boy, David Patrick, was born stillborn, the best support and comfort came from two women each of whom had lost a baby at birth, too. They knew the pain I felt. They offered their hands to me. No one can say words of magic to stop the hurting, but it helped to know there were others who had suffered as I had and were there for me.

The death of a baby is so horrible. People tend to stay away from those who lose a baby. It definitely is not a time to be alone. If you lose a child—although I pray not—please seek someone who can truly share your pain. There are support groups springing up across the country. Seek them out. Don't try to go it alone.

Margaret White, Ashley, OH

The death of a child has hit our family. Let me share some dos and don'ts.

Don't ever say, "You can have more children"; or "Thank heaven you have other children." This is cruel. The child's worth is not dependent on whether or not there are siblings.

Do mention something regarding the child's uniqueness—and they are all unique—his/her creativeness, his/her caring ways, his/her friendliness. Let it be known you will miss him/her also.

One more thing. Do encourage the mother and father to talk about their child during the months following. It takes two full years for grief to change to acceptance. Encourage them to join a support group: AMEND is for parents of a stillborn baby, and Compassionate Friends [P.O. Box 3696, Oakbrook, IL 60522-3696 (312) 990-0010] is for those suffering the loss of child.

C. Mallien, St. Louis, MO

For updated information on AMEND, SHARE, and other support groups, contact: National Self-Help Clearinghouse, 33 W. 42nd Street, New York City, NY 10036; (212) 840-7606.—Ed.

parents forum

Q How and when to tell a child he's adopted

As an adoption worker, I learned that one cannot underestimate the importance of "telling"—the earlier the better. The more naturally the information is relayed to the child, the less mysterious adoption will be.
Shirley Cohn, MSW, Burnaby, BC, Canada

Tell the truth—and as early as possible! My son loves the story!
Kathy Mellott, Rockville, MD

We are soon to be adoptive parents of an infant Korean boy. Since he's entering a ready-made family with a brother and sister older than he is, I'm sure he'll often hear about when we adopted him—and our trip to the airport to meet him as a family.
Terry Baker, Kirkwood, MO

From the moment we met our daughter (6½ weeks old), we used the word "adopted" in our songs and stories. When she was a toddler, we'd often ask, "Who's our adopted angel?" She enthusiastically called out, "Amanda!" As we wait for our second adopted child, Amanda (now 3½) sees firsthand the steps we must take to apply for and wait for her new baby brother or sister. She has already visited the agency and will join us when we bring home "her" new baby.
Valerie Frederick, Virginia Beach, VA

Remember—Superman was adopted!
Clark Kent, Metropolis, USA

We adopted a baby girl recently. We feel she will always know. She won't have to be told. Adoption is our way of having a family. Giving birth is another. Don't put too much importance on adoption.
Judy LeMay, South Burlington, VT

I was adopted and my parents handled it very well. We read books (THE CHOSEN BABY, for example) and were always told the truth. Our questions were always answered. The truth is the best—after all, there is no need to hide the facts. Adopting a baby is a wonderful thing.
Ellen Uzialko, Langhorne, PA

Our adoption worker and every book I read advised telling children immediately. Our children still LOVE to hear about it. I made a book of photographs with a simple story. As they grow older, I add the details that we know. Books that helped the most were IS THAT YOUR SISTER? (S. & C. Bunin, Pantheon, $4.95) and THE CHOSEN BABY (V. Wasson, Lippincott, $7.95). When they're older, I'll read HOW IT FEELS TO BE ADOPTED (J. Krementz, Knopf, $11.95).

We celebrate the day we adopted them with a special family dinner. Making the adoption known from the beginning helps everyone deal with it better. Somehow, making a big deal out of it means, in the end, that it's no big deal.
Sharon Amastae, El Paso, TX

Because we send pictures of our adopted son to his birth mom and have some contact with her through the lawyer, he will be exposed to the idea gradually and at an early age. He already "signs" a card to her for Mother's Day. We believe that the more open and honest we are, the less fear there will be. If we just "announced" it at some later date, it would be a big deal. Some good books I've read are WHY WAS I ADOPTED? (C. Livingston), AND NOW WE ARE A FAMILY (J. Meredith), and SOMEBODY GO AND BANG A DRUM (R. Caudill).
Debbie Parnakian, Huntington Beach, CA

WHERE TO START
National Adoption Hotline
202 463-7563
information and referrals

N. American Council of Adoptable Children
1346 Connecticut Ave. NW
Washington, DC 20036
referrals to local support groups

OURS is an organization that helps adoptive parents of transracial, foreign, handicapped, abused, and older children. They will supply information about local support groups in most states, and they have a 65-page bi-monthly newsletter ($16/year)
OURS, Inc.
3307 Hwy 100 N
Minneapolis, MN 55422

For information about helping adopted Oriental children adapt: ORIENTAL CHILDREN IN AMERICAN HOMES by Frances M. Koh ($11.45 ppd) Published by:
East West Press
PO Box 4315
Minneapolis, MN 55414
(612) 379-2049

What Do You Say When ...?
How do you respond when people ask personal questions about you and your adopted child? An adoptive mother, who's heard all the "stupid" questions people ask, gave these suggested answers in a DEAR ABBY column.

Q. Oh, isn't it a shame you can't have "children of your own"?
A. *Not really, there's a lot of insanity in both of our families.*
Q. Do you know all about the parents?
A. *Everything. One was male. The other was female.*
Q. Did the adoption agency try to match your features, coloring, and personalities?
A. *Good grief, I hope not!*
Q. Aren't you worried about hereditary factors?
A. *Heavens, no. Regardless of how bad their ancestors were, they've got to be better than OURS!*

Joey and his adoptive dad, Catholic priest Father Clements. Their story is one of nineteen warm short stories shared in HOW IT FEELS TO BE ADOPTED by Jill Krementz (Alfred Knopf).

parents forum

Q How have you helped with learning problems?

As a remedial reading teacher, I can't stress enough the importance of turning *off* the TV and turning *on* a good book! Read aloud with your child until the day he or she leaves your home! I heartily recommend Jim Trelease's *The Read-Aloud Handbook.*
Sue Chaplin   Toledo, OH

My son (almost 3) has to have his hearing checked because of ear infections. His hearing problem might be interfering with his speech. I try to talk clearly to him.
Ruth Metz   Rockaway Twp., NJ

Should I Worry Yet?

No learning-disabled child is exactly like another. Learning disabilities are not like measles or whooping cough: there is no one symptom to look for. Symptoms occur in clusters, which vary from child to child.

Some of the major symptom-clusters to watch for are: activity levels and attention (hyperactive or hypoactive children); movement and perceptual development (problems might be with coordination, vision and/or hearing, including faulty depth perception or the inability to coordinate information from different senses into a coherent whole); language and thought development (problems might include limited vocabulary, poor pronunciation; dyslexia falls into this cluster); and emotional and social development (problems in this category may be the result, not the cause, of learning disabilities).

If you suspect your child of having a learning disability, first try learning more yourself. Your local library or bookstore should be able to help you find one or more of the wonderful books currently available. Then, if your concerns seem to you to be well-founded, get professional help. Whether it is a pediatric neurologist, a hearing or vision specialist, a psychologist, or some other specialist, there is someone who can probably tell you what the problem is. After diagnosis, follow up with a program of therapy. Experts agree that the earlier you detect and treat a learning disability, the better are your chances that your child will suffer little or no adverse emotional, social, or academic effects.

I have held both children out of school an extra year in hopes of preventing problems. Both were immature, fall-birthday boys. The second has a speech articulation problem. He is now taking classes to correct it before entering kindergarten. He could not have handled phonics this year because he didn't say words correctly. We have never emphasized it, but we praise him when he tries hard and gets a word right. He loves class and is working hard. The older boy is doing great in first grade.
Jo Marshall   Fremont, CA

My daughter (6) and I did some catch-up reading during the summer. It was a fun but disciplined time.
Cindy Coppage   W. Hartford, CT

Once my oldest daughter's teacher told me she needed help with suffixes and prefixes. So I sat down with her. She didn't want to hear it from me at all! She said, "I'll ask the teacher."
MaryEllen Cooper   Glendale, AZ

My daughter (4) has delayed development. We have her in a wonderful program called Project Pre-dict!
Lynda Rubinson   Des Plaines, IL

Our daughter has difficulty pronouncing "l" and "w," so we designed some verbal exercises taken from Bert and Ernie on SESAME STREET: "la la la la, love you," "la la la la lollipop," "la la la la laughter."
Diane Sutton   Los Angeles, CA

As a former sixth-grade teacher, I advise parents to work with the teacher and help their children as much as they can. The problem doesn't go away, it just gets worse as they get farther behind.
Claudine Mitchell   Peculiar, MO

We switched to a private school.
Karen Haynes   Upper Marlboro, MD

Personal attention after school and lots of praise, support, and encouragement for good work.
Kathy Lord   Rochester, MN

Get a professional tutor!
Unsigned

First it's necessary to find out *how* the child learns: orally, visually, etc. Then proceed from there by devising aids that a teacher might not have time for. PATIENCE is required.
Cam Wilsie   Clio, MI

A child I tutored in English had a hard time learning contractions. I made charts that show the different parts of the words in different colors. For example, have NOT = haveN'T, you ARE = you'RE. [*We used capitals instead of colors. Ed.*] It worked wonders!
Michele Price   Alexandria, VA

Short positive sessions on a regular basis really helped. So did our Apple computer.
Margery Bartell   St. Louis, MO

Talk to a professional, because only he or she can give you the right approach to the problem. The most important thing to remember is to be reassuring to your child. Don't alarm him or her needlessly.
Nedra O'Neill   Evergreen Park, IL

My son is in a speech class working on "s," "z," and "sh" sounds. Every time he says a word using one of those sounds, I remind him of another word with the sound and note if he says it correctly. His teacher sends home suggestions, such as practicing in front of the mirror, which we all do with him.
Harriet Landry   Belford, NJ

We use a tape recorder. He enjoys recording, loves the sound of his own voice, and can take it to bed and listen to the lesson as he falls asleep.
Leigh Galey   Metairie, LA

parents forum

Q How do you handle custody and stepparenting?

I was divorced when my boys were 7½ and 10½. They see their dad for half of the summer, half of Christmas vacation, and at Easter. He lives in another part of the state. One of my boys romanticized the freedom there so much that we let him live there for 1½ years. He returned with the conclusion that all that "freedom" (lack of supervision) didn't make him feel loved. They know that when they get older they can live with him if they choose.

Barbara Wade Napa, CA

I was divorced when my daughter was 2½ years old. She's now 11½. Our custody arrangements looked great on paper, but my ex-husband decided not to abide by them and chose his own arrangements instead. He calls once a year at Christmas and demands to see her. I don't comply and he thinks I'm unreasonable. And he doesn't see how unfair he is being to our daughter.

Kathi Baldwin Rancho Cucamongo, CA

I have been divorced since Jessica was 18 months old. I have custody and her father visits her occasionally here at the house. She is very well adjusted. I've told her that our family may not be exactly like other families, but we *are* a family and we love each other and are happy, which is very important.

Judi Hoey Morristown, NJ

Don't belittle the former spouse to a child. An adolescent will despise you for it, and a younger child will be confused and unhappy. Remember, even if you and your new partner have custody and are paying all the bills, the parent who only visits has some stake in the child, too!

Unsigned

My children (12 and 14) stayed with me in their own house, in the same neighborhood with the same friends, etc. The effect was optimum stability in a very traumatic time.

Tine Thevenin Edina, MN

My sister is divorced. She had her two boys (9 and 13) in the beginning; then her ex-husband had them. When he remarried, the older boy moved with him and the younger stayed with my sister and her new husband. Both boys are very bitter and it's very sad. They love both their parents and are torn. The older one can't get along with his mother because he hates her new husband and they fight constantly. Both boys resent her new husband.

Barbara McGuire Wantagh, NY

I have two friends with unusual custody arrangements. In one situation, the two children (7 and 10) spend the school year with their mother and summers with their father. They love it. In the other, it's half a week with Mom and half with Dad. It's very traumatic for the children (1½ and 4). The younger one has problems with diarrhea and the older one has withdrawn into his own world.

Kathy Lord Rochester, MN

I am a stepparent of a 13-year-old with a 2½-year-old of my own. One of my pet peeves is comparisions by my stepson's mother between my son and hers. (Of course, her son is always better!) My stepson lives with his mother and her husband and comes to us for alternate weekends and some vacation time. His mother complains about the problems she has with him, and expects us to fix everything in the short time we have with him. We've offered to take him permanently but she refuses. We have discipline problems when he's here and are constantly reminding him about our house rules. My husband is torn between his two sons and is afraid of showing favoritism.

My advice? Try to have as little direct contact as possible with the other natural parent. Let your spouse handle that. Make the stepchild as much a part of the family as you can. Grit your teeth and bite your tongue when you have to. (Now if I could only follow my own advice!)

S. Skolnick Sunland, CA

My husband is the stepfather of my two daughters (7 and 4). I want to recommend two excellent books for stepparents: STEPPARENTING by F. Philip Rice, and THE STEPFAMILY: LIVING, LOVING, AND LEARNING by Elizabeth Einstein.

Patricia Berggren Hampden, ND

My husband and I joined a stepparent support group. I recommend it highly. If you can't find one, start your own!

Chris Shoop Metairie, LA

For information about finding or starting a support group, contact The Stepfamily Foundation, 333 West End Ave., New York, NY 10023 *or* The Stepfamily Assoc. of America, **602 E. Joppa Rd, Baltimore, MD 21204** They can help with other aspects of stepparenting as well.

Ed.

Helping Kids, Helping Ourselves

from Divorce Can Happen to the Nicest People *by Peter Mayle (illustrated by Arthur Robins)*

As parents going through the crisis of divorce, we often tend to buy books on the subject for our children even before we buy them for ourselves. I found that my children often did NOT like to read what I put under their noses, even though I thought I was being helpful. My suggestion would be to play it by ear. If your children are receptive to reading about divorce, fine. If not, hold off for a while; maybe a little later they'll be more able and willing to deal with it.

Everyone's situation is different, and of course the age of the child involved is also an important factor. If you think your child would like to "read more about it," here are some books you might consider.

DIVORCE CAN HAPPEN TO THE NICEST PEOPLE by Peter Mayle (Macmillan, $9.95). This large format, hardcover book was one of the few my children enjoyed. It's similar in style to other Mayle books; the illustrations keep it light and upbeat, and the text is realistic and reassuring.

GROWING UP DIVORCED by Linda Bird Francke (Linden Press/Simon & Schuster, $15.95) helps parents help a child through the predictable reactions to divorce that depend on the child's age and sex.

THE KID'S BOOK OF DIVORCE BY, FOR AND ABOUT KIDS by Eric Rofes (Random House, $3.95). This book can help parents understand divorce from a child's point of view. If you know what's most worrisome to your children, you'll be better able to help them cope. (This book is a bit too sophisticated for use with children under the age of 6.)

THE PARENTS' BOOK ABOUT DIVORCE by Richard Gardner, MD (Bantam, $3.95) discusses various approaches parents can take to help their children cope with the changes in their lives caused by divorce.

—VL

Q Have you suggestions for single parenting problems?

I remember how hard it was for my mom when my parents were divorced. A single parent should include the kids in as much as possible—it helps them feel part of a family and not that they are a burden and unwanted by the parent.

Bessie Dobbs, Lakeville, MN

My cousin is single and can see it would be best for her little girl to find a grandmotherly sitter instead of shifting her between relatives and friends when she goes out.

Mrs. Pedric, Eden Prairie, MN

Be honest and open with your children. Have a support system (friends, family). Realize that you can't be everything to your child.

Michele Chollet, Kansas City, MO

No experience here. (Sometimes I feel like I'm raising three children—our two little ones and my husband!)

Sarah Hoback, Albers, IL

I am a single parent, divorced. When my 3-year-old tells me he wants Daddy to come home, I tell him that Daddy is in Dallas working and that when he grows up and gets a car, he can go and visit Daddy. He really likes the idea of getting a car when he grows up!

Anna Hovenden, El Paso, TX

I feel like a single parent sometimes because my husband is gone a lot, working both full- and part-time jobs. I've found I have to be organized, yet flexible, when the occasion arises, and ALWAYS remember what my priorities are.

Cynda Thompson, Fenton, MO

Parenting is hard enough—doing it alone seems an impossible task. My hat goes off to each and every single parent!

Nedra O'Neill, Calumet Park, IL

Join self help groups and read everything that could help solve problems.

Barbara Declerk, Pocahontas, AR

Although I'm not really a single mother, my husband will be overseas for four weeks. The most important thing I've learned is to get out and get some adult contact—go to a friend's house or have her come to yours. I spent the first week alone with my 8-month-old daughter (not much company!), and when I went back to work it was like getting out of prison.

E. A. Johnson, Midwest City, OK

I don't have suggestions, but I surely do admire single parents after having spent several evenings alone with my 2-year-old. The 6 p.m. relief person sure is important!

Tina Rohde, Golden Valley, MN

DIVORCE PROBLEM NOT AS NEW AS WE THINK!

One out of every two marriages ends in divorce, yet the institution of marriage is booming. Such optimism in the face of such failure is a trend that began in the early decades of this century. In studying divorce records from the 1880s and again from 1920, Elaine May, a University of Minnesota professor, has discovered that contemporary confusion about sex roles in marriage is nothing new.

"I found that the common wisdom for the rise in divorces—the emancipation of women—was off the mark," May said in an interview. "Actually, the increase in divorces was linked to the greater interest in marriage on the part of both men and women."

Marriage gained popularity because it came to be considered more important to individual happiness, May said. The great expectations more and more often led to divorce.

It was different in the 1880s. "Marriage was based on duties and sacrifices, not on personal satisfaction." Husbands, above all, were providers, and wives filing for divorce were righteously indignant if they had been forced to work.

In the 1880s it was the men who were accused of overindulgence in amusements, while May's 1920 divorce samples showed twice as many women as men being accused of too heavy a night life. But as far as attitudes toward working outside the home was concerned, 1920 wives resembled their 1880s predecessors.

"Personal life seems to have become a national obsession in 20th century America," May writes. "It is not likely that the domestic domain will ever be able to satisfy completely the great expectations for individual fulfillment. As long as the American pursuit of happiness continues along this private path, divorce is likely to be with us."

Single Parents and the Holidays

The first holiday of your new family structure is the most difficult. That's the bad news. The good news is there is only one "first" time round. You'll survive each first holiday single and each succeeding year it will get better. Small comfort, I know. To turn the "lemon" into lemonade takes a bit of planning and effort. Don't carry the burden alone; share feelings with your children and let them help with a solution.

●Make decisions about "who gets whom" and "who goes where" as far ahead as possible, and tell the children, so they will know what they are doing. With teenagers, ask for their input, keeping in mind that they will want some of their holiday time with friends and without either parent.

●Celebrate the eve of the holiday at one home and the day of the holiday at the other. Children often like this best because they get double the holiday fun which makes up for what they have lost in family unity.

●Separate two children so they can share the holiday alone with one parent. You can switch midway through so each child has some time with both parents. We often put the burden of family togetherness on children by assuming that if they are together at the holidays then at least some part of the family is "intact." But children often enjoy being "singletons" and separating is also one way of ensuring that neither parent will be alone.

●Starting new traditions. Let your children help you come up with new ideas. Will it be caroling? Visiting grandparents or friends in a nursing home? If you always opened gifts Christmas day, open them on Christmas Eve this year. Go sledding New Year's Eve and make it a new annual event. Have the Easter egg hunt elsewhere.

●Don't be apologetic about making drastic changes in gift-giving habits and expensive celebrations, if finances are tight. Children enjoy making gifts and setting up new, less materialistic traditions.

The Single Parent Resource

Parents Without Partners, Inc. is perhaps the best known of the organized groups, with 1200 local chapters in the U.S. and in Canada and Europe. The organization offers social, cultural, and educational activities for parents and children. It publishes *The Single Parent*, a bimonthly magazine ($9/year).

For information write:
Parents Without Partners, Inc.
8807 Colesville Rd
Silverspring, MD 20910

parents forum parent

Q What do you think you did RIGHT

The most important thing I feel my husband and I have done right is to give our children a Montessori education. Not only is it wonderful for the skills they have learned, the independence, self-respect, self-control, and respect for others they have gotten, but because our home life reflects the same kind of atmosphere—calm (relatively!), peaceful, accepting, and respectful.

Mary Ellen Cooper, Glendale, AZ

A goal for my children was to have them enjoy books *forever*, so we began reading to them early (3-6 months). They are only 2 and 4 now, but adore them, watch little TV, and even can occupy themselves alone "reading." It's paid off, and I am so pleased. We've learned lots, too.

Ida Sorensen, Cedar Rapids, IA

I think my kids have learned to be supportive of anyone with a problem—even me! They have all learned to be wonderful listeners (they hardly *ever* tuned in to me in matters of neatness, however!), and emotionally are very warm. I hope they got some of this from me—but their dad is super in this respect.

Merrie Ann Handley, Boulder Creek, CA

The best thing that has happened for my children is to have a mom who doesn't need to be and doesn't expect to be liked by the kids all the time. Also, letting them know right where they stand...with love, rules, consequences, and so forth. No guessing games or assumptions.

Sharon Stitt, Seattle, WA

I really had to stop and think here. First of all, what's right? I have shown lots of love and caring, which seems so important. After that, I'm not sure. There's no true test.   *Debbie Ulrich, Lewiston, MN*

I think I've kept my expectations and limits appropriate to the age of my child. Not only is that kind to your child, but also makes life easier on parents.

Francie Gass, Bellingham, WA

We watch our children and meet their needs as it suits them. If you listen to them and your instincts, you can't go wrong, whether it deals with weaning, toilet learning, or whatever. Also an informed parent is the best parent. I read all I possibly can.

Donna Holmes, Perry, OH

Taking time every day to make time and to genuinely be enthused by doing something they love—biking, a long walk, playground, clay, paint, games. And I don't slack. I participate fully with all my attention. They are so much more loving and patient afterward.

Janice Holden, Ocean City, NJ

I have learned to express appreciation for what is done right and have learned to expand my patience when things are going wrong.

Erde Sun, Philomath, OR

Not being wishy-washy in decisions is extremely important. Kids pick up on that weakness immediately!

Gail Caso, Elmer, NJ

I think one of the best things to teach children is manners (please, thank you, I'm sorry, and so forth). Mine aren't always courteous to each other, but are around other people.

Marlene Gwiazdon, Osceola, WI

One thing I've instilled in my children is honesty. I have yet to hear any of the three in an out-and-out lie—even when it warrants a punishment because they've done something they shouldn't have done.

Sharon Beyer, Milwaukee, WI

1) Teaching the children that having emotions and feelings and expressing them in constructive ways is good. 2) Reinforcing good self-esteem. 3) Having a relationship with God is an important foundation to life.

Dana Clark, Santa Barbara, CA

Kept a positive attitude—kids are easygoing and happy. As parents, we are flexible and so are both kids.

Mrs. John Watson, Great Falls, MT

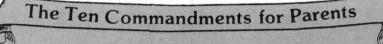

The Ten Commandments for Parents

1. I will appreciate each of my children for what they are, not for what I want them to be.
2. I will relate to each child as an individual, instead of "the kid."
3. I will take good care of myself as a person, so as not to smother my children as a parent.
4. I will acknowledge each and *every little* acceptable behavior, and not just the "biggies."
5. I will give my children as many "facts" as I am able and trust them to weigh these facts and make responsible decisions.
6. I will not allow my children to use or abuse me, for I know this will damage *them*.
7. Knowing that my children are on a short-term loan to me, I will introduce them to every possible responsibility, so that they won't be too shocked at "independence."
8. I will let my children know that I love them unconditionally, whether I like their decisions or not.
9. I will allow my children to face the consequences of their own actions and not to constantly protect them, as I know I will want to do.
10. I will feel successful when I am no longer needed as a parent.

forum parents forum

as a parent?

from *Do They Ever Grow Up* by Lynn Johnston

I love my children—just like I want them to love me. Golden Rule, I suppose.

I enjoy the hell out of parenting! I like everything about little boys—frogs, Great Danes, lizards. Am I overdoing it?

Kathy Hickok, Delray Beach, FL

I try always to respect each child's individuality and differing needs. Often that means lost sleep or not going out or just not getting to do what I want at the moment. I feel that if I respect them now they will respect my wishes (a little more!) later.

We always tell our children how much we love them and praise whenever possible.

Judi Welsh, Apple Valley, MN

I love my kids. I think as a result they're loving persons in return—to me and to others. I think this unconditional love from both parents also has allowed them to be independent thinkers with self-confidence. (Hope you never ask what I think I've done wrong, though!)

Karen Gromada, Cincinnati, OH

Love isn't what you feel, it's what you do.

This may bring a flood of letters, but I think the best thing I've done for my kids is staying home with them. We have sacrificed a *lot* by my not working, but I know, deep down, that it is so worth it. We may not have the beautiful new car we had when Ryan was born, or a lot of other things, but we do have extremely happy and well-adjusted kids. Not to say those children of working moms aren't, but this is the best thing I can do for my kids, in my opinion.

Sandy Heath, Brownsville, TX

I don't know what we did, but our 4-year-old son is kind, honest, and gentle. Our 6-month-old has been sleeping through the night for four months now. I wish we knew what we did right with her, so that we could bottle it and sell it!

Maryann Shutan, Highland Park, IL

It's important to make them feel loved at all times, even when they do something wrong. The message to get across is that the *action* or *deed* is under disapproval, not the child.

Billie Salas, Albuquerque, NM

If you bend over backward for your children, you will eventually lose your balance.

I think the most positive thing I have done is to decide not to have any more children! I *thought* I could handle at *least* six children. After three children in 3½ years, I saw reality. At that point, it was either sink or swim, and since I decided to "swim," I armed myself with as much information on children, parenting, and other related topics as possible—and I have made it!

My main guideline is remembering that my three children are not "kids," but "little people" who deserve the same respect and courtesy that I pay adults.

Nedra O'Neill, Calumet Park, IL

I think I try hard to treat my kids and babysitting kids like people, not "little kids." I try to understand how they feel, or their side of the story. I hate hearing people talk down to kids like they're dumb because they are little. Kids have opinions and feelings, and I try to hear them out, not force my opinions or ideas on them.

Mrs. Tom Jacobsen, St. Edward, NE

Two things we have done that I think made the difference are:

1) Starting from birth we'd hold them and tell them we love them when they are happy (smile), sad (frown), laugh, cry, wet, dry, dirty diapers, dirty, clean, sick, well, when they make a mess, inside, outside, up, down, reading a book, playing, asleep, awake, eat, drink, and so forth. Saying "I love you when . . ." before each word or phrase keeps their attention for minutes at a time. My 2-year-old will come to me now and say, "Laugh, cry," so I will do it. If we are somewhere we have to wait, I do it when I think he's getting restless, and he calms down and listens to every word. If you personalize it to fit the child he knows you watch his activities during the day. My 7-year-old still loves to hear it!

2) Following *their* lead—not what I think they should be interested in. David, so many times, will say, "Mom, how did you know this is what I wanted?" My 2-year-old loves clocks. He now knows his shapes because I draw them with a clock inside each. I think this makes them feel that we do notice what they like and will try to help whenever we can.

Other little things we do that help: Noticing when they do something by themselves; letting them eat without criticism; putting them to bed and saying, "Gosh, we have such good boys (even if it's a bad day!) after we close their doors but loud enough for them to hear; and, of course, giving them lots of affection when they (or we!) need it. *Pat Hart, Chesapeake, VA*

I've been here. Loving and steady. I had her at age 44 and was ready to enjoy everything about parenting. I could feel the love for her going like water to roots. Of course, it helps she has turned out healthy (51 inches, 73 pounds at age 6!), a strong, intellect, beautiful—and sweet! *Unsigned*

I think I've done the right thing by simply being there for my two preschoolers. It's been hard. My professional life was much easier, and I miss it. I tried part-time work, but the preparations for it were overwhelming, and I gave it up. I look forward to returning to work when the going gets easier. It will, won't it?

Pat Brinkmann, Palo Alto, CA

The only thing I'm positive about is that I'll have to wait for the kids to grow up and *tell* me! *Marjorie Rennett, Beverly Hills, CA*

Why can't I think of the many things I've done right when both children are crying, supper is burning, and I would give anything for a nap? *Unsigned*

parents forum parent

Q What would you do differently

I would throw out all the books and just relax and enjoy!
Sharon Scranton   Bellflower, CA

I would be more consistent with discipline. I find myself getting angry with my children because *I'm* not clear about what I expect from them. I wish I was more fair more of the time.
Nedra O'Neill   Calumet Park, IL

I would accept each stage in a child's development for what it is, and not be in such a hurry to go on to the next stage.
Karen Bowen   Sandwich, IL

My biggest regret is all the times I've said, "Not now, I'm busy." I realize that my children will remember the time I've spent with them, not the clean house and elaborate recipes.
Becky Gammons   Beaverton, OR

I yell at my kids too much. When it's one on one I remain very calm, but when it's two against one, I lose my patience and yell. Even if I tell myself I won't do it, I still do. Unfortunately, they both yell a lot, too.
Jeanne Gretter   Sigourney, IA

LETTING GO

One of the hardest parts of parenting is learning to let go of our kids and let them grow up. What exactly does it mean to let go?

To let go does not mean to stop caring; it means realizing you can't do everything for your child.

To let go is not to cut yourself off, but to learn that you can't control anyone but yourself.

To let go is to admit powerlessness, which means the outcome is not in your hands.

To let go is not to try to change your child, but to accept him or her as is.

To let go is not to take care of, but to care about.

To let go is not to fix, but to be supportive.

To let go is not to be protective, but to permit your child to face reality.

Author unknown

I might have had children earlier if I had known how much I would enjoy being a mother.
Linda Haugen   St. Paul, MN

I would have spaced my last two children at least three years apart. Fourteen months is much too close. Now they're good playmates, but I feel my middle child got cheated out of her babyhood. She had to grow up too fast.
Sharon Beyer   Milwaukee, WI

I was too strict with my first child.
Anna-Maria Hertzer   Kensington, CA

With our first child, I always made sure he was asleep in my arms before I put him to bed. He slept poorly until he was two. With my third child, when it's bedtime or naptime, I just put her to bed. My blood pressure is a lot lower!
Janet Gift   Davis, CA

I would have held them more. I didn't learn to treasure those precious early months, and I feel my first three children suffered because I was too busy cleaning and reading about childrearing or comparing my kid to other kids. Use your time to love them.
Darla Penny   Superior, WI

I would have listened to *no one* giving advice, and subscribed to PRACTICAL PARENTING instead. Follow your own good instincts and let your children be who they are. Love them and accept them. Take each day at a time. They do grow up too fast.
Kris Gialdini   Fremont, CA

With my oldest I worked full time plus and I missed a lot! I would never do that again. He's 5 now and clings to me a lot. I think I overcompensated when I wasn't at work; I was overprotective and doted on him.
Mona Hanlin   Hartland, WI

I would not try to be so perfect and demand such perfection in my firstborn. As a result, he is anxious in new situations and worries about doing things "right."
Ann Jordan   Blue Ash, OH

I did not say no often enough. I gave in to them after they whined or pestered me. I should have been stricter with them.
Marilyn F. Baumert   Herndon, PA

I would give my child more space to be himself instead of being scared of what I think he's going to do.
Cindy McCormack   Phillipsville, CA

forum parents forum

as a parent today?

I didn't recognize that I didn't need to please everybody with my or my kids' behavior. Disapproval was deadly to me, and I never seemed to be able to do the right thing. My kids took the brunt of my unhappiness with myself.

Merrie Ann Handley   Boulder Creek, CA

I would fret less, worry less, yell less, clean less, buy less, and expect less. I would play more, kiss more, understand more, praise more, and defend more.

Marcia Len   Cohoes, NY

We haven't had the kids help out around the house enough. It's far too easy for me to do my thing while they play than to organize them into helping with chores.

Jodi Junge   Bryn Athyn, PA

When we bought our house, I wish we had better researched the quality and proximity of educational and recreational facilities, and the "expandibility" of the house to accommodate more than just the two of us, the amount of traffic on the street, etc.

Phyllis Engart   Willow Grove, PA

I fed my firstborn commercial baby food almost exclusively from 6-14 months. I then found she was unwilling to accept any rougher-textured food. I should have advanced to "people" food at the first sign of readiness.

Cynthia Coppage   W. Hartford, CT

I wish I had let my children do more for themselves. It is still hard to realize that they are getting older and more independent.

Maureen Deitsch   Toledo, OH

I didn't allow my firstborn to handle the baby much and kind of kept them apart for fear the baby would get hurt. Now I think those relationships and feelings are more important.

Linda Merry   St. Louis Park, MN

I had a gut-level feeling that my daughter should wait a year to start kindergarten, but we let her go early. Now we're considering having her repeat. It's difficult because her friends will all be going on to first grade. If only we had waited!

Mary Kowalski   DeKalb, IL

I would hire a babysitter for daytime relief. I feel I would have been a better parent if I'd had some breaks from the constant demands.

Lucy Barcelo   Ithaca, NY

I wish I hadn't started out yelling. They don't listen anymore. I wish I had sought help sooner for my son's learning deficiency.

Jerri Oyama   Northridge, CA

I get angry and yell a lot. I'm not very understanding about constant spills and messes.

Joy Goldwasser   Denver, CO

I'm learning the most important rule, consistency. My 4-year-old reminds me all the time, "But how come you let me do it yesterday?"

Blythe Lipman   S. Windham, ME

I would read all about the baby *before* it came. Make an effort to touch a baby, babysit, talk to parents. I was completely bewildered when the baby arrived—a colicky one who never slept at night. But I can finally look back and laugh and see it as a maturing process. But there was one time when I could have killed the baby and myself!

Connie Tenn   West Linn, OR

I would have spent more time away from my son in the earlier years. I trusted only my mother to watch him and didn't leave him much as a baby. Consequently, separation was much harder for both of us later. I'm sure he sensed my apprehension and we both suffered from it.

Susan Skolnick   Sunland, CA

I'm afraid other people (sitters) had too much influence in the upbringing of my children because I had to work full time. I wish I could've worked part time.

Monica O'Neil   North Liberty, IA

I think my biggest mistake was forgetting to take time for myself and my husband. If any more children enter our lives, I think we'll arrange for a sitter to come on a weekly basis.

Donna Poplawski   Houghton, MI

Begin from infancy to give your child everything he wants. In this way he will grow up to believe the world owes him a living.

When he picks up bad words, laugh at him. This will make him think he's "cute." It will also encourage him to pick up "cuter" phrases that will blow off the top of your head later.

Never give him any spiritual training. Wait until he is 21 and then let him "decide for himself."

Avoid use of the word "wrong." This will condition him to believe later, when he is arrested for stealing a car, that society is against him and he is being persecuted.

Pick up everything he leaves lying around. Do everything for him so that he will be experienced in throwing all responsibility on others.

Let him read any printed matter he can get his hands on. Have no concern whatever for what goes into his mind. Let his mind feast on garbage, and let his brain drink out of any dirty container.

Quarrel frequently with your spouse in the presence of your child. Then he won't be too shocked when the family is broken up later.

Give him all the spending money he wants. Never let him earn his own. Why should he have things as tough as you had them?

Praise him in his presence to all the neighbors. Show how much smarter he is than the neighbor's children. Take his side against neighbors, teachers, policemen. They are all prejudiced against your child.

When he gets into real trouble, apologize for yourself by saying, "I never could do anything with him."

Prepare for a life of grief, because you will surely have one.

John Winters Fleming

parents forum parent

Q Would you have children again, if you "had it to do over"?

I definitely would; my husband feels differently. They have enriched my life tremendously. Though my husband considers children restricting, he admits he can't imagine life without them.

J. Oyama, Northridge, CA

Yes. Maybe not three, but definitely one. Nowadays it's hard to support more; seems both parents have to work to make ends meet. I wouldn't take a million for the three I've got, but you couldn't give me a million to have another.

L. Smith, Roscommon, MI

Most definitely! Children have given me the opportunity to truly "grow up." I stopped being a child when I had a child.

Dawn Lee, Orland Park, IL

Yes! But we waited eight years, got many "wild oats" sowed beforehand and discussed at length the lifestyle change we would face.

Lynn Bradford, Huntersville, NC

Yes! I never thought that two little people could bring out the best and worst in me. I couldn't imagine, nor would I want to, being without them. Who else could make me laugh and cry at the same time?

Bobbie Spallina, Oak Lawn, IL

It makes me feel sad that some would not have children again. We only regret that we can't afford as many as we would like. I wish anyone with doubts of wanting a famly wouldn't have one. I believe there would be many more happy children.

Gail Schutz, Whitehall, IL

I would again have children, but I would do more reading and observing on the subject before the children were born.

Nedra O'Neill, Calumet Park, IL

My marriage would have been happier without children, as I have realized that my husband is a workaholic. Two workaholics without children works. However, I thoroughly enjoy my children and do not regret motherhood.

Laura Kory, Fairfax, VA

NEVER! I love my 8-year-old, but I've learned that I'm not naturally good with children. Wanting to be something doesn't mean you become it instantaneously.

Mary L. Gerald, Rochester, MI

After only six months, perhaps I'm not entitled to say. It's been four months of colic, two colds, an ear infection, a month of 24 hours a day in shoes and a bar splint and, of course, teething. But I'd do it over in a heartbeat! I think nothing could ever compare to the wonderful experience of her birth, until as she wakes each morning and I enter her room and a smile bursts on her face like sunrise—and I know no one ever was or will be happier to see me.

Fern Nogowski, Nashua, NH

YES! I have gone through the stresses of losing one child and dealing with a serious illness in another, but the rewards have been more than worth the hardships endured.

Cathy Kienzle, Bow Island, Alb.

YES, YES, YES! But we'd have started sooner. We were 33 when our first was born.

K. Hickok, Delray Beach, FL

I've been poundering the question for almost six years now, ever since my colicky first-born son covered me from head to foot with regurgitated formula. I wondered about why people have children when he got me in the face as I was changing his diaper and sweetly singing to him. The question crossed my mind again as my husband and I rushed him to the hospital in the wee morning hours, nearly sliding off the icy February road, after he'd had a febrile convulsion.

I think I found the answer to my question today. After a walk with the family, I started thinking about all the fire engines I'd waved to in the past six years, all the low-flying airplanes I'd greeted, all the "choo-choo" trains I'd pointed out to the kids. I thought about how much fun it was to play with the sandbox the first time we set it up and what great sport it was to splash everyone with the water from the pool.

Children add a fresh, new and exciting—albeit exhausting—dimension to life. I am beginning to think that one of the reasons, conscious or not, that people have children is so that they can experience the world as children just once more.

Excerpted from a column by Didi Mann in the "Neighbors" page of the Minneapolis Tribune

---

The LADIES HOME JOURNAL recently took a poll of some 30,000 of its readers and found out the usual things about love, fidelity and its crashing bore of an alternative, infidelity. It also found out some interesting things about children. They tend to sour a marriage.

Ann Landers found pretty much the same thing when she took a readers poll some time back. Her readers said that if they had it all to do over again, when it came to children, they wouldn't do it. Other polls have found the same thing and not only when it came to women. Men, too, feel that children can put the kibosh on marriage or, to quote the psychologist Nathanial Brandon, "make it harder for a marriage to proceed happily."

It is as though some people think that to acknowledge the problems children can cause in a marriage means, somehow, that they don't love their own children or they are conceding that they made some sort of terrible mistake. This may not be the case at all. What is the case is that the first step towards dealing with a problem is simply to acknowledge that it exists. Freud said that—or should have.

This, after all, is what we have done when it comes to marriage. The same should be true when it comes to children, but that is not yet the case.

The truth is that children change relationships, and not always for the better. It is important to realize that. After all, children are involved.

Excerpted from a news story by Richard Cohen in the WASHINGTON POST, reprinted in the MINNEAPOLIS TRIBUNE.

forum parents forum

Yes, definitely! I never realized how wonderful having a child was. Our daughter is only 2, but she has added so much to our lives. The three of us enjoy our times together and sharing our lives with each other. The love and friendship that has developed is something I would never trade.
Linda Haugen, St. Paul, MN

Yes! Beware, though, if you don't want a child, don't have one. I'm a nurse and have had my fill of unloved children.
Barbara Headman, San Francisco, CA

I would. When my 20-year-old sister was killed in an accident, my mom and dad said it's harder to lose a child than a spouse—children are a part of you. God puts a child in your protection to love, guide and enjoy for as long as we can, even after its death or ours.
Cathy Wiese, Glendale Heights, IL

YES. Before the children came, I worked full time. I felt that all I was doing was working, sleeping and eating. But now, despite its certain routines, each day is different and rewarding. My life is much more fulfilled.
Cynda Thompson, Fenton, MO

I enjoy every minute with my 7-month-old daughter. I believe it helps that we waited five years before she was born and that I'm 26. Also, I read everything I could get my hands on before we had her, and that helps.
K. Murray, Milwaukee, WI

Definitely yes. It's like Kahlil Gibran's passage about love. Without children, "you will laugh, but not all of your laughter and weep, but not all of your tears."
Linda Brunn, Denver, CO

On days when the sun is shining, the kids healthy and happy and the house generally at peace—YES. When everyone is at each other's throats and I haven't slept for three straight nights because someone is sick, I wonder if I wasn't crazy to even start a family, let alone have five children. In all honesty, although the hours stink and the pay is non-existent, I would jump at the chance to do it all again.
Catherine Poulos, Park Ridge, IL

We had the chance to start over when our 11-year-old daughter, an only child, died. We lived the next two years in the most incredible loneliness—and silence. Not to do it over again! Who could say a thing like that! I don't understand.
Mrs. S. McClelland, Park Ridge, IL

I would definitely do it over. We are broke—the loss of my income hurt—things are always a mess—but I cannot imagine life without my children. Maybe the fact that I was 35 when I had my first has something to do with it. Before, I traveled and did many things. I don't feel tied down or that the "outside world" must be so exciting. My inside world here is more exciting.
Harriet Landry, Belford, NJ

Parenting can be a lot of fun . . .
. . . IF you can stand the children.

It's a very normal feeling to want to return the merchandise and I'm having those feelings right now! I do not want an exchange . . . I do not want them credited to my account . . . I just want my money back!

I didn't get a warranty against defective parts or a guarantee that I wouldn't hear bad-mouthing or a certificate of cleanliness. In fact, I didn't even get a chance to fill out an application. I can't take the shock of one of my offspring showing up for dinner after three years of being a mystery guest. I object to spending nine-tenths of my income on my children . . . I want it ALL for myself.

I resent the constant driving of little people to and from the dentist, the emergency room, the ski slopes, the ball field, school, scouts, the hairdresser, the beach or the local precinct. I find it nauseating to discover six years of dirty socks, petrified peanut butter sandwiches and milk glasses with the hairy, green, culture on the bottoms—all filed under the beds.

The thought of having a garage WITHOUT piles of bike parts, skis, mufflers, oil cans, swim fins, jars of grasshoppers, potato chip bags, roller skates, kittens, skate boards, tools, stashed homework and more moldy sandwiches would be too much to take!

This is what parenting REALLY is!

Gee, that felt good! Now that I have that off my chest, think I'll go home and plan a special taco dinner . . . the kids love 'em. Hope the kitchen hasn't been condemned by the Health Department.

(Signed)
PARENTS EVERYWHERE
Reprinted with permission from THE PARENT PLACE, Seattle, WA newsletter.

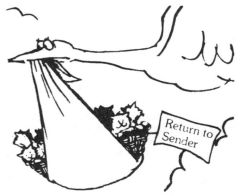

parents forum *parent*

Q What is the best parenting

Twenty years from now they won't remember how clean the house was, but they will remember that you had time to read to them and play with them.
Chris Palagallo   Peoria, IL

Love your children for who they are, not who you want them to be.
Kris Gialdini   Fremont, CA

It was from the front feature ("Neatness *Doesn't* Count") of the Jan/Feb '85 issue of *Practical Parenting!* My mother kept trying to tell me that, but reading it seemed to pound it in. Thanks!
Gina Zager   Naperville, IL

My aunt told me it's okay to wish your child didn't exist (just sometimes and only for a moment). I was shocked! Now that I've been through the terrible twos, I know what she meant!
Terry Saevig   Van Nuys, CA

Babies need lots of love. They need to be talked to, played with, danced with, and sung to. They *don't* need a bath every day, to cry themselves to sleep, or a lot of fancy clothes and equipment.
Anne Kuhlman   Woodville, OH

I wish I had believed people when they told me not to pick up my baby every time he went boo. By the time he was 6 months old I was his slave!
Linda Card   Boca Raton, FL

I believed that you *could* spoil an infant. Wrong, wrong, wrong! I found with each additional child that the more contact (both physical and verbal) I had with them as an infant, the better we *both* felt. Don't be afraid to meet your child's needs. The result is a very secure adult!
Nedra O'Neill   Evergreen Park, IL

When your child is deliberately trying to get a rise out of you by doing something bad, don't say one word, just pick him up and put him in his room or in a special corner. And if he gets up before you want him to, put him back, but don't say a word.
Julie Bowman   El Toro, CA

Don't ever say that you will *never* do something!
Alice Horne   Norcrosse, GA

Go with your instincts. You know your child better than anyone else does.
Mary Enriquez   Santee, CA

Don't try to be too fair or even things out— you never can. Each child needs different things, and each needs time alone with you.
Harriet Landry   Belford, NJ

One day at a time!
Diane Spizzirri   Schaumburg, IL

When your child is acting like a 2-year-old, try not to act like one yourself.
Debbie Megginson   Auburn, IL

Parents need to be united and in charge.
Kathy Lord   Rochester, MN

There is no one right way to parent. Consistency and love are the most important things.
Nancy Miller   San Pedro, CA

Be flexible. *Very* flexible!
Lil Schulman   Burnsville, MN

That it's okay for me to say no or to give an order—without explanations, guilt, apologies, or bargaining—simply because I am the mother.
Myra Weaver   Hollywood, FL

You need patience and a willingness to get down on the floor and play with your children. Also, if you treat your child with respect, he will do the same with you and others.
B. Bird   Hilton Head Island, SC

forum parents forum

advice you have ever received?

As they grow, give them freedom without pressing them into a mold. Let them be themselves.
Fran Heydenburg   River Grove, IL

Expect a child to do his best in everything he does and you will never be disappointed.
Margaret Kunc   Schwartz Creek, MI

Happy parent, happy child. Leave well enough alone.
Karen Burkland   Sherman Oaks, CA

Be *consistent* according to the age of your child. Being wishy-washy in discipline does not make a good parent—or child!
Kathy Skelton   Two Harbors, MN

On the way home from the hospital with our new baby, my husband said, "Relax, enjoy, and remember that things can't be perfect. You'll drive yourself crazy if you expect everything to be perfect."
Cathy Petrovich   S. Lyon, MI

Each child is different, so try not to compare. This puts less pressure on you and your child, and it gives your child a greater sense of self-worth because you like him just the way he is.
Marjorie Rennett   Beverly Hills, CA

Children survive all your mistakes. They are very forgiving and resilient. So much of the guilt parents feel about not being perfect is unnecessary.
Sue Johnson   North East, PA

From a mom who raised two brilliant girls: "Don't try to rush the stages a child goes through. Just let them be kids. Their time is so short." Thank you and I will.
Karen Gay Leitch   Singapore

Be good to yourself! Only when your cup is filled can you nurture others.
Jane Hietbrenk   Corona Del Mar, CA

I just read *How To Talk So Kids Will Listen and Listen So Kids Will Talk* by Faber and Mazlish and it has changed my life! It's full of great advice.
Also, my mother told me that infants are boring and it's okay not to be fascinated.
Unsigned

Love never spoils a child. And listen to your kids, because one day they just might stop talking if you don't.
Jeanne Fedoryshyn   Palm Harbor, FL

Don't take everything to heart! What seems like a major problem now will in six months have you wondering why you were so worried about it. Kids change quickly.
Donna Schreier   St. Paul, MN

Forget about stages and "when is he going to do such and such?" and just enjoy your own special little person. And try to keep things in perspective. A day of non-stop crying is usually just that—*one* bad day—not a new schedule for the next three months!
Kathy Croom   Virginia Beach, VA

I read it just this week in your newsletter in a Parents Forum answer from Sue Howard: "let your child be a child, not a small adult." It really make me stop and think. I wish I'd heard it a few years ago.
Linda Zatarski   Frankfort, IL

"Try to rest when he rests," a quote from my dear mom!
Sue Chaplin   Toledo, OH

Read to your children for at least half an hour *every* day.
J. Dawson   New York, NY

When my daughter was going through a very aggressive stage, my pediatrician told us to stop emphasizing discipline and emphasize love instead. Spontaneous and frequent affection work better than any three minutes in the chair!
Susan Keck   Gaithersburg, MD

Read as many books on parenting as you like, and listen to all the advice, but then do what *you* feel is right for your child.
Christy Schmidt   Kerkhoven, MN

Allow and encourage your children to cry and express their emotions. We spend far too much time distracting them and not allowing them to vent.
Michele McBrayer   Georgetown, KY

Direct your child with positive statements instead of negative ones.
Francie Gass   Bellingham, WA

Put yourself in your child's place once in a while.
Karen Haynes   Upper Marlboro, MD

The best advice I ever got was from a woman whose child had died. She regretted every extra meeting, TV show, and phone conversation that seemed so important at the time and kept her away from her child. I've made a conscious effort to stop saying, "Not now, I'm busy" because the time you have to enjoy your children is just too short.
Gina Walker   Hickory Hills, IL

The piece of advice that meant the most to me was this: "Parenting skills have to be *learned.*" It really took the pressure off once I realized that just because I'm a parent doesn't mean that I will always know the right thing to do.
Anne Schuster   St. Paul, MN

I view parenting as a benevolent dictatorship—I save democracy for the federal government and other idealists!
Vicki Lansky   Deephaven, MN

Nobody Told Me There'd Be Days Like This. . .

My toddler is 10½ months old. Today she learned how to open the lid on the 40 gallon garbage can and deposit her new Christmas toys inside. Yesterday she learned how to open the dryer door and let the cat in. This afternoon she realized that she can stand up unaided on the seat of her rocking chair—and rock. Earlier this morning she unrolled two rolls of toilet tissue. As soon as I see her turn her back to me, I make a mad dash; she's usually furtively popping something disgusting into her mouth (rug fuzzies, wadded paper scraps, cooled cinders from the fireplace, the cat's dry food pellets). These days. . .I'm mostly tired!
Jackie Haag   Holden, MA

parents forum parents for

Q Are kids personality traits

look! she's got a temper just like you!

from *Hi Mom Hi Dad* by Lynn Johnston (Meadowbrook Press)

Having two children that are so very different has convinced me that they are born with certain personality traits. We certainly have some control, but some days I don't think I have very much!

Susan Barnett   Waco, TX

I was very concerned about the effects on my first child of a pregnancy filled with stress and grief (both my mother and mother-in-law developed and died of cancer during that time). However, she was a "good" baby, and at 2½ remains calm, happy and good-natured. My second daughter is different—more physical, independent, and confident—and I sensed the difference immediately after delivery.

Barbara Kreski   Oak Park, IL

I have always believed that the pregnancy, labor, and delivery have a lot to do with the child's disposition, and in turn their personality. One daughter is hardest on my nerves of all my children, and her pregnancy was hardest on my body. Her delivery was marred by nervous, over-worked nurses and a too-quick labor. She needs much more reassurance to remind her she is just as special as her brother and sister.

Nedra O'Neill   Evergreen Park, IL

Born, born, born! They learn courtesy, discipline, appropriate behavior, etc., but how and when they dish it out is organized in their little DNA ladder when the egg and the sperm first say "hello." I think you have about as much control over your kids' lives as you do your own (which is very little, most days, in my experience).

Maureen Morriston   Ft. Mitchell, KY

The more experienced I become as a parent, the more I see how my children are like me or my husband—it almost scares me. I think our lives as children are just extended a little through our own children.

Maureen Deitsch   Toledo, OH

Children are born with personality traits. The challenge of parenting is to see how well our own personalities get along with our children's. That is the deciding factor in "successful parenting." Her basic personality doesn't change, but as I learn more and more about my daughter, my parenting changes.

Karen Haynes   Upper Marlboro, MD

I believe children imitate their parents to a large extent. What you believe, do, and feel often transfers to your children when they are young. When they get older and as their outside contacts broaden, friendships outside the family become increasingly more important and influential. You try to instill basic values in your children and hope when the time comes they can make the right choice!

Anne Moore   Columbus, IN

Both. My son is now 20 months, and I think I will have a lot of control over how he turns out. Ask me again when he's 16 and I will probably have a different answer.

Connie Waddington   Seattle, WA

It's definitely a combination of influences. I can already see that peer influence is very strong, but it's important to try to control who they spend a lot of time with.

Lynn Naman   Houston, TX

I think some personality traits are inborn. For example, my son is a human snail—everything he does, he does slowly. I noted this in his baby book when he was 2 days old, and it hasn't changed. I've tried bribes and threats but he can't speed up. I do feel children can be molded somewhat, especially by being exposed to different experiences.

Unsigned

Definitely! I have two kids raised the same way and they're as different as night and day. I think it's wonderful to believe so, then I won't feel so guilty.

Connie Tenn   West Linn, OR

Children are born with certain character traits which can be molded to some extent. I commend the book *Your Child Is A Person* (Penguin, $3.95). It reminds us our children are unique individuals.

Karen Drotzer   Croton-on-Hudson, NY

am parents forum

molded or inherited?

My son has 75% of his father's and grandfather's personality. Yet *I* am the one he is around 75% of the time. I was raised by an aunt, but I have my mother and father's personality traits, and my aunt's "values."

Claudine Mitchell Peculiar, MO

I have come to believe it's a combination of both. To believe that you can mold a child is to assume that you can dictate all that your child thinks and does—which, obviously, you cannot—not if you want your child to be independent, creative, and capable of making decisions on his own. I'm trying to create a positive environment for my child, help him develop a positive self-concept—that, I believe, IS in a parent's control. There are many terrific things in *every* child. A parent's role is to see what's terrific and encourage it!

Mrs. Metzger Miami, FL

Yes, they are born with their own individual dispositions, but parents set limits and guide them into acceptable behavior. I don't believe you can change their basic natures, but you can help them cope to some extent, and channel their energies. Lots of love, respect for their abilities and opinions, and firm guidelines can do wonders. Lots of patience helps, too!

Jo Marshall Fremont, CA

I think a "good" child can be ruined by a parent, but a difficult kid is probably difficult no matter what. My son has been easy since birth. Even now, in the middle of the "terrible twos," he is not awful. I don't think its because I'm a great mother, rather it's the way he came. I think parents have control over their children's values (in the broadest sense) but not their personalities.

Joanne Shawhan Delmar, NY

I think a child is born with a personality, a learning style, a developmental schedule, self-esteem, and a desire to grow. My parenting controls his emotional development more than his physical or mental development or his personality. My parenting will mostly influence his basic feelings for his life, and his ability to reach his potential. It will show in his coping skills.

Sarah Schiermeyer Weston, MA

I believe genetics plays a bigger part in our lives than we'd like to admit.

Karen Henry Broken Arrow, OK

This answer seems to cover the majority opinion:
I think it's half and half. Your child is how he is, but he certainly can be brought up right or wrong. You can give your child the basics, but it's up to him how he will turn out.

Kris Taranec Lake Havasu City, AZ

I firmly believe that children can be molded by good parenting, and they are born with certain personality traits. I find it interesting that when children grow up to be happy and successful, everyone compliments the parents on what a good job they did. When children grow up with lots of problems (drug abuse, delinquency, etc.) everyone says it's not the parents' fault! You can't have it both ways. Let's take responsibility for our children's upbringings, no matter what.

Marsha Mood Janesville, WI

Since my 2-year-old was born, my husband and I have often commented on how much he acts and looks like his 4½-year-old half sister. It's amazing that two children with different mothers could have so much the same personality traits. My husband's genes must have something to do with it. Since the children only see each other for 1 month a year it couldn't be from anyone's "molding."

Maureen Fernandez Las Vegas, NV

Children are natural mimics: they act like their parents in spite of every effort to teach them good manners.

I do belive they are born with certain traits. Both of mine seemed to have distinct personalities in utero. I believe molding exists only to socialize the children.

Susan Wells Rockwood, IN

I believe a portion of each child's personality must be inherited (such as active or passive), but I don't think a child is born with self-esteem or the ability to love and share and be a good person. Those traits must be learned.

Vicki Piippo Richland, WA

Myth: *Personality is set at birth.*

By Joseph Rosner, Ph.D.

Fact: Personality is *not* set at birth, although children may be born with definite temperaments. Studies do show that at birth there is the easy, adaptable baby, the hard-to-adapt baby, and the slow-to-warm-up baby. Whether these temperaments become pronounced or are almost extinguished depends on the home environment of the baby. The person who influences the baby's temperament the most is the mother. Long-term follow-up studies have found that the rigid parent and the hard-to-adapt baby have the most difficulty in adjusting, and in such cases, instinctual temperamental inclinations become part of the child's permanent personality. In reality, personality grows in the individual as a learned response to the accumulation of life experiences, beginning at birth and continuing throughout life.

Both human and animal babies *are* born with primitive, instinctual defenses, which nature intended as protections against danger. The human brain retains this ancient animal or jungle brain, but adds the dimensions of an intellectual brain. The old brain is the seat of the emotions, while the new brain is a learning brain that allows us to progress far beyond the primitive lifestyles of our ancestors.

While certain instincts may be stronger or weaker in individual babies, it is the degree to which the environment arouses particular instincts that will have the greatest influence on personality development. If the environment is calm, supportive, loving and responsive to the baby's needs, the baby will be able to thrive, to gain security and trust to develop a positive outlook on life, and to develop intellectually. If, however, the environment is tense, cold, rejecting, and unresponsive to the baby, all the primitive survival instincts will come to the fore, leaving tension, rage, fear, panic, and feelings of desertion in their wake. Instead of thriving, the baby will be subject to digestive upsets and illness; instead of developing security and trust, the baby will learn insecurity and mistrust; instead of optimism, pessimism will grow; and instead of being free to develop on an intellectual level, the baby will continually be overcome by emotions that will restrict his functioning to a very primitive level.

The earliest experiences will have the strongest influence in shaping personality. This is probably why the myth of inherited personality originated. Parents will often note that a particular child has been basically happy or irritable, friendly or fearful, "ever since he was a baby." This may refer to the fact that the baby's temperament may be set at birth and that the child's overall experiences early in life helped foster a particular personality pattern.

Myths of Child Rearing (Dembner, $8.95)

parents forum

Q How have children changed your marriage?

We talk less and stick to basics: kids, bills, fixing the roof. When we're alone, we tend to stare at each other and wonder where the conversation went.

Jo Marshall Fremont, CA

We go more places because there are things we would like the kids to see and do. There is some sacrificing of privacy, though.

Jane Davidson Falls Church, VA

Freedom. We can't do whatever we want anymore. Financially, the kids are a strain. Emotionally they are all-consuming. They've made our marriage stronger because we share them as the most important things to live for. As for each other—who has time?

Ellyn Okrent Lauderhill, FL

Our first child drove a wedge between us so deep that seven years and the next child later, we're *still* trying to get back together emotionally.

Cheryl Kronberger Oak Park, MI

Before our son was born my husband and I led pretty separate lives. Having a child forced us together, and for the first time we became a "couple." Now he's not only my husband, he's my best friend!

Jane Larrabee Beverly, MA

We don't have the time (or energy) for trivial fights. We appreciate each other more.

Cindy Kubick Lincoln, NE

Immense strain. So little time to hold and hug one another. Even after 17 years of marriage, having our 2-year-old calls all our supposed "strengths" into question.

Diane Wolcott Castro Valley, CA

We can't pick up and go on the spur of the moment anymore. Everything costs more. Our candlelight dinners are punctuated by flying food occasionally and whining constantly. We think in terms of "family" instead of "couple" now. Mostly, we have a new and immense goal to accomplish together—raising responsible, loving children.

Rene Kehrwald Spokane, WA

The biggest change I've noticed is the amount of work there is to do: extra cleaning, clothes washing and folding, etc. I don't have the spare time I used to. Emotionally, I feel my ability to love has expanded. The love you have for your children is phenomenal! I would do anything for my son.

Debbie Haag Costa Mesa, CA

You learn that you must grow up and be responsible. You are no longer "free" to do as you please. I learned this; my husband didn't. He found out that he didn't like being a father and left us for a new girlfriend so he could be "free."

Kris Taranec Lake Havasu City, AZ

There are a lot more smiles! We were very career-oriented until this bundle of love came into our lives. Now we have redirected our goals as a family.

Kathy and Tim Wilson Mound, MN

The most difficult change was that we had different ideas about how to parent. I was pretty strict and my husband had an "anything goes" attitude. We finally took a parenting class, did lots of talking, and are beginning to meld together so that we aren't at odds. Things go much more smoothly now.

Diane Abell Loogootee, IN

The sense of REAL responsibility. And a reason to live our life to the fullest, to enjoy life with our child.

Gail Goldberg Northridge, CA

Our respect for each other has increased because we see the other trying to be a good parent.

Sally Sellers Grosse Pointe Park, MI

We are closer than we had ever imagined possible during the six years we were together without kids. Parents experience the highest highs and the lowest lows of every possible emotion.

Belinda Stanley Conroe, TX

Before children, I felt if things got bad and I was unhappy, I was free to leave. But now, things would have to be impossible for me to deprive my girls of their father.

Debbie Lutz Baton Rouge, LA

My husband feels the most significant change is the larger role he plays in our marriage. He feels he participates more in household chores and also communicates his needs more.

Joan Schulen Chicago, IL

We have had to make a special effort to spend time as husband and wife, not exclusively Mom and Dad.

Christine Koning Piscataway, NJ

Sticking together is easy when love is the glue.

Never before have we had so many disagreements and rather intense discussions. Most of these conflicts have something to do with the kids.

Lita Crocker Rossford, OH

Financially it has been hard, but emotionally it's even harder. We love our daughter so much that the marriage comes second, which is very bad. We are finally adjusting.

Alice Horne Norcross, GA

The lack of spontaneity for *anything*. Remember last-minute movies, spur-of-the-moment brunches, last-minute weekends out of town, sex whenever (and wherever) you wanted? Now I feel like General Patton moving the troops when we plan a trip to McDonald's; every last detail needs to be planned or we might not survive!

Pat Spiker Columbus, OH

The birth of our children has given us insight into our own values and morals. We have learned a lot about each other through our children.

N. Webb Toronto, Ontario

FATIGUE!!...........zzz

N. Wright Houston, TX

from It's Another Baby! *cartoons by Neil, Marion Books,   PO Box 415, Greensborough, 3088, Victoria, Australia.*

parents forum

Q Dad: How are you different from your father?

Vastly different! Dad believed that "children should be seen and not heard" (and preferably not seen). I'm winging it. I've read, I've seen what I *don't* want, and I'm out there doing what feels right. Family involvement is a high priority for me.

Bill Whitlock Northampton, MA

My father has an even temperament. He very seldom yelled or spanked. I'm less patient. I often wonder how he kept his temper with all of us (three).

Unsigned

I stay home with the children and my wife works. It was a mutual decision. The two children go everywhere I go, and they see me doing most of the housework. I am trying to set a good example for my children, unlike my father, whose philosophy was "do as I say, not as I do."

I try not to spank except for very serious infractions. My father was a strict disciplinarian who used a belt all the time. My parenting style is totally different from his.

Charles Richardson Ft. Defiance, AZ

I have a more personal relationship with my children. My son spends a lot of time with me around the house working, and I cook with my daughter.

Bernie Landry Belford, NJ

Nothing is the same! Because we both work, we have no time for the male role of head of the household. I do all the cooking because I have a more flexible schedule. We have two girls. I change them and bathe them, and I feel very close to them.

David Schweyer Detroit, MI

My father traveled a lot, so we never developed a close relationship. I am self-employed, which allows me to be at home every day and to participate in my son's life every day.

Steve Lincoln Ramona, CA

Being married to a childbirth educator has made me more aware of the father's role and the importance of bonding by *both* parents—something considered unmanly in the "old" days.

Tom Imhoff Cincinnati, OH

My father was very much a nurturer and very affectionate with my brother and me. Occasionally he still calls me "honey" without noticing. As a result, I'm very close to my children. (P.S. My brother and I are both normal, heterosexual males with stable marriages and two kids apiece. We weren't "warped" by his cuddling and affection.)

Larry Stanley Conroe, TX

I don't think he rolled around on the floor as much as I do, or had very much one-to-one contact with me. That was the 50s, you know.

Joe Day Boulder, CO

My son has a father who is more aware of talking about feelings, etc.

Rick Witucki Rochester, MN

My wife and I occasionally work opposite shifts. I have spent two to three days a week alone with Jonathan (20 months). My father only saw us in the evening.

Gary Schutkin Glendale, WI

My father was typically old-fashioned. Anything concerning child raising was my mother's responsibility, NOT HIS! I'm so glad I belong to a new generation of fathers who understand how vital it is to devote as much personal and play time to their children as possible. My fathering style is based mainly on my experience as a child, growing up with a father who cared but didn't show it. It may sound strange, but my best role model has been my wife. She has showed me that a father can do almost any parenting task that a mother can do.

Bob Ludwig St. Charles, MO

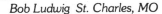
Don't be the man you think you should be. Be the father you wish you'd had.
Letty C. Pogrebin

Today's Father

Today, 8 out of 10 hospitals in the United States allow fathers in the delivery room. 85% of fathers choose to be present during labor, and 50% attend the delivery. When the father is present, delivery time is shorter, anesthetics are used less, the mother and baby are calmer, and feeding problems are less likely to occur.

Fathers are closer to their children these days, and the nurturing father is a new kind of role model. Fathers and mothers have become more equal partners in parenting. Research shows that when fathers are active with little children, the children get along better and do better in school. When fathers play with children, they touch more and talk less than mothers do. They smile more, and they tend to play more physical games. Obviously, children benefit most from the active involvement of *both* parents.

American men are working hard to avoid repeating what they view as the mistakes they saw their own fathers make. Their increasing parental involvement presents its share of problems, and many men are experiencing the pull between work and family for the first time, something women have had to deal with for a long time.

Here is how one father expressed the challenge of fatherhood:

I was going to be the perfect father: loving, caring, nurturing. I was going to make up for all the men who leave the children to the women, who back away from intimacy with children, who are cold and distant. I was going to do it right.

Tonight I saw how scared I am. There is so much to do for this little creature who screams and wriggles and needs and doesn't know what he needs and relies on me to figure it all out. Part of me wants to get as far away from him as I possibly can.

He's only been here a month, and already it's more than I can handle. I finally admitted how far I am from where I would like to be.

I tried to tell my wife what was going on with me. It felt good to confess, to break down.

Afterwards I had the beginning of a new vision: I need to accept my fear, my reluctance. I have to start from where I am instead of where the model new-age father would be.

I am so small compared to what needs to be done.

from Fathering: It's Not the Same, *The Nurtury Family School, 374 West Baltimore, Larkspur, CA 94939, $11.95 ppd.*

I allow my children their independence. I share experiences rather than taking over.

Robert Cianciulli Miami, FL

I'm a much more active caregiver than my father was. Childcare duties are divided more evenly.

Unsigned

I spend more time with my family. Other than that I think I'm pretty much like him. I hope so; no one could care more than Dad does.

John Bengson Russell, KY

parentsforum

Q How do you handle "Do as I say, not as I do"?

My belief is that children will copy whatever we do and very rarely what we say. If there is something I positively do not want my children doing, such as lying or stealing, I would *never* allow myself to do it in front of them!

Mary Ellen Cooper, Glendale, AZ

It's very embarrassing to me, so I try to avoid being in a position where I have to justify my actions at all costs.

Susan Wlodek, Jackson, MI

There are many things adults can do that children can't. I explain that to my girls, and tell them that when they are adults, they can decide for themselves—but as children, they have to obey a stricter set of rules.

Sandi Mink, Detroit, MI

When I scream because they're screaming, then I calm down and describe how frustrated I felt.

Shirley Cohn, Burnaby, BC, Canada

I think that quote should go down the toilet! How can we expect our kids to do as we say—and not be good examples ourselves?

Marcia Len, Cohoes, NY

When my kids ask for a taste of my wine or coffee, I just reply that when they get older, they may indulge. That usually satisfies them.

Sharon Beyer, Milwaukee, WI

It's been a very effective way for my husband and me to "clean up our acts." I wear my seat belt now, and my husband's grammar has improved. I don't believe you can ask a child to do something that you're not willing to do. I want my children to be able to respect me and my word.

Unsigned

When I affectionately pat our children, the gesture is sometimes returned more vigorously (smacking my back for instance). We talk it over, discussing *intent*. It may look the same to *them*, but the messages are very different.

Jodi Junge, Huntingdon Valley, PA

As our oldest is only 3, we haven't dealt with this yet, but I get the feeling that he's just *waiting* for the chance to jump up with a big "A—HA!"

Sandy Heath, Brownsville, TX

I'll be looking forward to others' ideas on this. I *often* find myself shouting, "Don't shout!" or lecturing, "Don't stand in front of the refrigerator with the door open!" or "Don't leave things around!"

They ask, "Why can you shout, leave the refrigerator door open, and leave things around?"

"Because I'm your mother!" just doesn't make it.

Jerri Oyama, Northridge, CA

Children Learn What They Live

If a child lives with criticism, he learns to condemn.

If a child lives with hostility, he learns to fight.

If a child lives with ridicule, he learns to be shy.

If a child lives with shame, he learns to feel guilty.

If a child lives with tolerance, he learns to be patient.

If a child lives with encouragement, he learns confidence.

If a child lives with praise, he learns to appreciate.

If a child lives with fairness, he learns justice.

If a child lives with security, he learns to have faith.

If a child lives with approval, he learns to like himself.

If a child lives with acceptance and friendship, he learns to find love in the world.

Dorothy Law Nolte

I handle it with one statement: I am a grown-up; you are a child. Although I try not to get into these situations.

Betsy Ratcliff, Newark, OH

I still bite my nails at 30, I'm ashamed to say. My 5½-year-old daughter has started and can't seem to stop. The only way she'll quit is if I do, I'm sure!

Janice Holden, Ocean City, NJ

We have told our 5-year-old to stay clear of our automatic garage door when it's closing. One day, when I closed it from the inside and then quickly ran out under it as it was closing, my son reprimanded me, telling me how dangerous that was and that I shouldn't do it again.

Pat Brinkmann, Palo Alto, CA

I was raised this way, and I think it really is a poor attitude. This is one thing I swore I wouldn't do myself. I'm sure there may be exceptions—we aren't perfect. But I can remember hearing that phrase *often* and grew up resenting it.

Vicki Piippo, Richland, WA

The biggest problem I can think of is trying to explain to our intensely logical 4-year-old why he must go to bed at 8:30 when he knows Mom and Dad stay up much later. We haven't solved that one satisfactorily yet.

Becky Wilkins, Lubbock, TX

At dinner, when salt, pepper, or other things are used that I do not permit Susan to use, I tell her it's only for grown-ups. I am firm about that, and she accepts the explanation. That goes for ashtrays, magazines, or books that aren't hers—and anything else that applies.

Joanie Ecker, Foster City, CA

My older little girl is very much like I was as a child in temperament, habits, and in vulnerability. So, when I see her do something I instantly recognize as "me" that I want to change, I have to be sneaky—or honest!

Belinda Stanley, Conroe, TX

Unfortunately, they have heard us (occasionally) use words they are not allowed to say. When caught, I admit it wasn't proper, but also say that certain things that adults do are especially unattractive when done by a child.

Myra Weaver, Hollywood, FL

I see my children as little mirrors that reflect and copy the things that I do and say. When I don't like what I see, I change my behavior. When my 4-year-old catches me doing or saying something that she's already been corrected for (or knows better), then she corrects me and I have to say, "I'm sorry, that was a no-no."

What it comes down to is they teach me, and I teach them. We adults need to be their good example, because kids always have many of the same habits that their parents do. I see it in myself, and I see it in my parents, too.

It's our responsibility to train up a child the right way—and that starts with ourselves.

Pam Huntsman, Emerson, IA

Always tell your children the truth. They probably won't hear you anyway.

parents forum

Q Have you comments–pro or con– on the "only child"?

My husband is an only child and I swear, God willing, we will have more than the one we have. His parents are so dependent on him, FOR EVERYTHING. In fact, that has been the biggest bone of contention in our relationship. They call almost every day, even though we live 300 miles away. I will NEVER inflict such woes on mine.

No name, please

As the parent of one child (we planned it that way), I have found much support and research-based vindication in ONE CHILD BY CHOICE, by David Knox and Sharryl Hawke (Prentice Hall, $3.95). The authors furnish statistical evidence that in these times of inflation and overpopulation, the single-child option should be considered by every couple. The single child is likely to have a higher IQ and better verbal skills than children from multi-child homes and to be successful in school and generally self-confident and resourceful. S/he will probably be equal to children with siblings, if not superior, in emotional and social development. Your marriage is likely to be less strained than that of a couple with more children, and your home will be quieter, more orderly and more affluent. Best of all, perhaps, your relationship with your child will be close and intense. My husband and I feel that the advantages of having just one child far outweigh the drawbacks of not conforming to the mass-media image of the "ideal-two-kids-one-of-each."

Franceine Rees, Greenville, NC

Having only the one child now has made me appreciate how much my parents had to give up with their family of eight.

No name included

I'm so glad the spoiled, lonely only-child myth has finally been proven wrong! As an only child, I was neither spoiled nor lonely. My choice to have more than one was certainly not for that reason. I must admit it is very difficult for me to relate to my children's sibling rivalry.

Mrs. G. Oyama, Northridge, CA

I am an only child and decided I definitely didn't want the same for my first. It's lonely, sometimes boring and frustrating. However, on the plus side comes the seeking out and cultivation of true, meaningful friendships (no doubt because of a void there), which I feel particularly blessed with.

Pat Wickness, W. Vancouver, B.C.

People think if you have only one child you're selfish. In this age of energy and other shortages, I think people who have very large families are the selfish ones. Good book: RAISING THE ONLY CHILD, by M. Kappelman (New American Library, $1.95).

Mrs. C. Berra, Fenton, MI

I was an only child and hated it. My parents were 35 when I was born and so were always older than other kids' folks. They were loving and doting and stern—but I sorely missed siblings—and still do! I vowed if I should ever get married I would have a houseful of kids.

Jann Brewer, Marco Isl., FL

I have mixed feelings. As an adopted only child I was miserable. My worry-wart parents worried me to death. But when I look at my 7-month-old son I'm afraid that if we have more than one child I won't have time for the second and/or third.

K. Richardson, New Orleans, LA

I have an only child and am also a single parent. Although single parenting is hard, I think it's harder with one child. You have only each other and it's tough. Also, if you live in a neighborhood without appropriate playmates you play a lot of baseball, etc., which gets old quick. I think more is better, but not too many more. I wish I'd had twins.

Michelle Chollet, Kansas City, MO

Only children we know seem to have very high potential, but there is a sadness of not having brothers and sisters to share with. I don't think only children like the whole world of home centering around them. Too much pressure.

Mrs. Pedric, Eden Prairie, MN

I need another one to love! I feel I'd do too much for Bethany if she continued much longer as a only child.

Patti Welch, Rochester, NY

I personally feel it can be lonesome for an only child, but realize it's "none of my business." It can be due to choice, death of another child or children, adoption and inability to get more children, sterility of either parent or other personal reasons. If we who have more than one child probe the parent of an only child, we are digging into forbidden territory and deserve any response we get.

Carol Kenzy, Sunbury, PA

Intelligence and Family Size

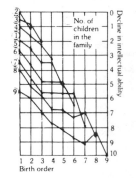

"It is well known that personality and intelligence are influenced by heredity, environment, education and child-rearing styles," writes Susan Goodman in YOU AND YOUR CHILD (Rand McNally, $14.95), "but they are also affected by the size of the family and a child's position in it."

Everyone won't like—or even agree with—the findings the author cites, and of course there are always exceptions. Research indicates, however, that the brightest children are those who are born first in small families, and that only children come in after these.

The ideal position, it's been deduced, is first of two children born closely together. One reason advanced is that the older has a chance to teach the younger, and is thus helped in development of verbal and reasoning skills.

Four reasons for the declining brightness of children born later in the family, as shown in the graph above, are:

• Each additional child depreciates the family's intellectual environment;

• Children from large families spend more time in a world of child-sized minds;

• The resources of a large fmaily, including income and parents' time and attention, are spread more thinly;

• Diets, understandably, may be less nutritious in a large family than in a small one.

What is an "only child?" I have five who all think they are the "only child!"

Catherine Poulos, Park Ridge, IL

I wouldn't want to be one and I wouldn't want to raise one. My sisters are my closest, dearest friends.

Sarah Hoback, Albers, IL

I never think of my status as an only child until someone starts to discourse on the subject in my presence. I think the topic of only children is overrated.

Pat Brinkmann, Palo Alto, CA

parents forum **paren**

Q How do you keep your kids

We make up crazy menus for our next meal, such as tree bark juice and peacock feather soup, which makes my son hysterical with laughter. Talking about what we will do when we arrive helps, too. Overreacting to the fussing *never* works. Keeping calm and reassuring the child does.

Jan Fraccaro Western Springs, IL

We set a good example by putting on our own seatbelts. When my son and I are in the car, I point out kids in other cars who aren't restrained (unfortunately, there are a lot of them). He feels sorry for them and calls their parents "dum-dums."

Linda Richardson Phoenix, AZ

The vision of a dead child is more than enough to make my insistence on car seats firm whenever we go out on the road. The children know I'm serious and rarely balk. One of my car seats is particularly hard to belt up, but I know I could never live with myself if that one-in-a-million accident happened. It's worth the few seconds of trouble.

Wendy Martin Havana, IL

As a childbirth instructor, I spend some time talking about the value of car seats. I point out that most couples are willing to spend a lot of time choosing just the right crib, but usually spend much less time looking for a car seat. I point out that their baby will be in the car seat far longer than in the crib. It's worth some extra time and money to get a good one.

Phyllis Engart Willow Grove, PA

On long trips, I take a bag of goodies: a new book, Colorforms, a small chalkboard and colored chalk. We bring food. Yes, I've been known to use a cookie or two as a bribe. We also play games, like every time you see a certain object (a blue car, a cow) you laugh. This gets my 3-year-old giggling in no time. We also sing a lot, and I mean *a lot*. If worst comes to worst, I pull over and calm them. Then back in the car seats and back on the road.

Betsy Jacquez Cincinnati, OH

My daughter loves rock and roll. So I turn on the car radio and she has a blast as long as there's a song on that she likes.

Cynthia Gillian Texas City, TX

We stress the importance of Mommy or Daddy being able to concentrate on driving at all times. It distresses me to see otherwise intelligent, concerned parents still not using car seats.

Unsigned

Unfortunately, the thing that makes them the happiest is gum and food— the messier the better. By the end of the week, the back seat and floor of the car could easily feed a family of five. If no one's screaming or fighting, who cares?

Cynthia Carlton
Los Angeles, CA

My job is to drive safely, not to babysit. I am increasingly immune to screams or complaints from children I know are safely secured behind me.

Elizabeth Benefiel
Tokyo, Japan

We use a large cloth bag to store favorite books and a few small toys. The handles fit over the head rests and the bag is suspended within easy reach of the car-seat riders.

Terry Baker Kirkwood, MO

My husband and I designed and built wooden folding lap tables. They have masonite surfaces for rolling toys and molding edges to keep cars from rolling off. They fold out flat so they can be stored easily. The kids also like cassette tapes of Raffi (the best children's folk singer) and stories, etc. The Fisher-Price barn and the Sesame Street Clubhouse are great in the car.

Tupperware has several helpful products: sipper seals for cups and containers (for raisins or goldfish crackers or pretzels).

Mary Kowalski DeKalb, IL

We won't start the car to go "bye bye" until my son is in his car seat, and we pull over and threaten to go home if he tries to get out. One sudden stop convinced him of the necessity of car seats much more clearly than my threats did.

Maureen Morriston Ft. Mitchell, KY

Until he was 2, my son would cry or scream whenever he was in his car seat. NOTHING amused him. Long trips were impossible. Short trips were long enough! Now, our persistence has paid off. He climbs into his car seat happily and reminds us to buckle up!

Linda Newberry Jermyn, PA

The Boy Who Wouldn't Buckle Up

Have you ever heard the story of the boy who wouldn't stay
　All buckled in his seat belt when his mother looked away?
Once he opened up the seat belt and climbed upon the seat.
　He knew he shouldn't do it, but he thought it would be neat!
He leaned way out the window as far as he could lean.
　He knew that it was wrong to do, but he was feeling mean.
When his mother hit a bump, this reckless boy fell out.
　He landed on the roadside and gave his head a clout.
He looked around the roadside, not knowing where he was.
　His poor head felt as if some bees had crawled inside to buzz!
"Oh me, oh my!" this bad boy groaned, "I'm lucky I'm alive.
　But how will I get home again with no one here to drive?"
He thought of all the many times he'd been told to buckle up.
　He knew that if he'd minded, he'd be home now with his pup.
The tears began to trickle down his dirty, muddy face.
　"If ever I get home again, I'll sit still in my place.
I'll keep my seat belt fastened and won't poke my head outside
　Of any car I ride in, no matter where I ride."
His mother quickly missed him and came back to pick him up.
　He sure was glad to see her, and soon he'd see his pup!
And ever since that scary day, no matter where he went,
　When he was told to buckle up, he gave no argument!

Betty Winn Fuller (reprinted with permission from *The Parenting Press*)

"It worked for me, and it can work for you."
Vicki Lansky's Practical Parenting

TRAVELING WITH YOUR BABY

forum parents forum

happy in car seats?

We keep a toy tied with yarn to my son's car seat so he can play with it when he's not looking out the window.

Pam Holbrook Pomona, CA

For long trips, I make sure they are dry, comfortably dressed, well fed, and approaching naptime before setting out. Then they usually fall peacefully asleep, and we're all happy!

Helen Parljuk Hastings, MN

Each of the kids gets to take one toy and may play with it as long as the belt is buckled on the seat.

Becky Wilkins Lubbock, TX

My daughter loves Mother Goose tapes by Melody House and WEE SING Children's Songs and Fingerplays by Pamela Beall and Susan Nippi, complete with book and cassette.

Unsigned

My son was "programmed" from infancy that we buckle him up because we love him. No lengthy explanations, bribes, or scenes. He likes to hear me ask, "Why do we buckle up our baby?" so he can answer, "Because we love him!"

Susan Skolnick Sunland, CA

I take crayons and paper, Etch-a-Sketch, and Magic Slate. My son also sings or shoots his imaginary gun at bad guys chasing us.

Claudine Mitchell Peculiar, MO

We saw a film on TV about car safety. A station wagon just like ours was used as an example, with dummies riding in the back. When the car was rear-ended, the dummies flew out the window. After that, our kids never gave us a hard time about wearing seat belts.

Amy Phillips Park Ridge, IL

I honestly never had a problem with any of my children being happy while buckled up because it was never a subject that was open to question. Quite simply, if we are in the car, we are buckled up. The key is consistency. I tell them we buckle up because we love them too much to take unnecessary risks. Remember: it's no fun to hear a child cry because he has to sit in his car seat, but it's a lot worse to have him die in a car accident and never hear him cry again.

Millie Tucker Roswell, GA

Our 2-year-old became attached to a blanket at an early age, so we decided right away to buy two identical ones. We keep one in the car and one in his crib. The first thing he does when we buckle him up is reach for his blanket. If we drive for any length of time he always falls asleep just as he does in his crib.

Sharon Scranton Bellflower, CA

We got an elastic cord with hooks on each end (like the ones you use to strap gear on a motorcycle) and stretched it between the clothes hooks on either side of the back seat. We can then tie soft toys within reach of the kids' car seats.

Pam Pitchford Albuquerque, NM

Kids usually hold out as long as the snacks do. Grapes, apple wedges, cheese cubes, pretzel sticks are not messy and don't hype everyone up. However, I admit to buying Tootsie Roll Pops and M & Ms as bribes. Colorforms are great to stick on car windows. I think long trips are insane with active children until they're about 3 or 4. They want to move their bodies. Explore your own state on mini-vacations until longer rides are more tolerable.

Karen Gromada Cincinnati, OH

Getting out of the car seat when the car is moving has never been an option for our kids. If they find out that fussing sometimes gets them out, they have an incentive to keep on fussing.

Natalie Warren Columbus, OH

BUCKLE UP YOUR BABY! *

Safety belts, safety belts,
Wear them all the way,
Every time you're in the car
Any night or day—oh—
Safety Belts, safety belts,
Put them 'round your lap,
Then before you start to ride,
Everybody—SNAP!

National Safety Council

(*to the tune of* Jingle Bells)

I point out trucks to my son and he talks nonstop about their color, size, contents, etc. I make sure his car seat is raised high enough so he has a clear view out of his window. My 1-year-old is afraid of traveling at night, so I place his car seat beside me up front and open the glove compartment. It has a small light inside that serves as a night light.

Janet Stabile Ellington, CT

If children don't know there's any other way, they will accept it. I brought mine home from the hospital in a car seat. My son hated being in the seat at night, so we got a small flashlight for him after I finally figured out that car and street lights were scaring him.

Michal Doesburg Orange, CA

I have always stressed the importance of buckling up, and I knew my son had fully accepted it the day he buckled his teddy bear in.

Cheryl Routh Las Vegas, NV

parents forum parent

Q Have you found good ways to make the punishment "fit the crime"?

Before I figure out if the "punishment fits the crime," I try to remember if the act is a crime—or merely a stage in my child's development. Louise Ames and Frances Ilg have written some extremely helpful books on just what to expect from different ages.
Jill Heasley, Fresno, CA

I TRY to punish with a slap on the hand for hand-related "crimes" or on the leg for leg-related "crimes", and so on. But I WON'T slap mouths. Any solutions for back talk, spitting and such?
Jerri Oyama, Northridge, CA

Duplicating the crime for the child helps increase understanding better than words or any other punishment (biting, slapping, hitting). Making the child clean the mess he created himself, turning off the TV or taking away the object being argued over by two or more kids all work. Grounding (making the child stay inside house or yard) works wonders for future compliance when the crime is running into the street, not coming when called, not coming home on time or going somewhere without Mom's permission.
LSM, Phoenix, AZ

I am so glad to see this! I wish more people would use this instead of automatically spanking. Every problem has a different solution. For example, after pouring out a bottle of bubble bath at a friend's house, my son had to give all his bubble bath to the friend to replace that which was wasted, and he went without any for a while.
Gail Schutz, White Hall, IL

I try to remember the "crimes" and will not allow the activity the next time, with a remark like, "maybe you can try chewing gum tomorrow. I picked up too many gum wrappers today which should have been put in the garbage."
Mrs. Joseph Miles, Champaign, IL

I've found one effective treatment for situations involving two or more kids when I don't know exactly what happened (which seems to be a lot!). I put them to work. If they won't work, they sit, secluded.
Patricia Schultz, Oak Park, IL

"The eighth deadly sin of parenting is to get yourself in a position in which you cannot make good your threat."
Erma Bombeck

Often I let my 7-year-old son implement his own punishments, which takes Mother out of the picture as "the old meanie." Many times he's much harder on himself than I would have been. It also seems to keep him from doing the same thing again. I do not use this for all punishment, but occasionally finding a punishment mutually agreeable keeps the home from being a dictatorship (run by either child or parent!).
Patty Turney, Houston, TX

I try to offer a choice, even if one of the consequences is artificially imposed by me. "You may pick up this toy and put it where you can get it, or I'll pick it up and have to take it away for a day or so." This seems to work well; I don't have to yell or repeat, and we each know the consequence. (Beware of setting a consequence that is harder on you than on the child!)
Cynthia Pring, Elbert, CO

David Lock (Exley Publishing, UK)

I'm now a mother, but I remember from my former teaching days an idea a retired teacher gave me. I had the kids write sentences I made up on the spot to fit the crime.
Claudine Mitchell, Peculiar, MO

Before I react to a "crime" I try to stop to think, "Was this a catastrophe? Is it worth blowing my stack over?" This usually puts the "crime" into perspective and I find I handle the problem with a little more self control.
Cynda Thompson, Fenton, MO

Using play equipment improperly or dangerously = loss of use (time based on "error"); being rude to friends = not being able to see them next time; loudness = time alone, quietly; littering our home = yard cleanup.
Deidre Schipani, Ellicott City, MD

My 5-year-old usually goes to bed at 7 p.m. because he has to rise early for school. Friday nights he's allowed to stay up until 10 p.m. if he behaves in school and at home. Usually the threat of losing a Friday night is enough to handle all the problems. Find some reward (even if it's not YOUR favorite) the child would die for—take it away once—and that may be the secret.
Mrs. P. Hart, Chesapeake, VA

You rip your brother's shirt, you give your brother your shirt. You take "my" toy, I can take "your" toy.
Mrs. K. M. Claseman, Maplewood, MN

I have a 5- and a 6-year-old. When they were younger I would always pick the punishment, but now that they're older and since they know my ways of punishment, I make them choose their own punishment. These range from no dessert for table incidents to giving up a toy for a week for not sharing.
Cindy Lennon, Burnsville, MN

I find when I get mad I think much more clearly if my child is in his bedroom, "thinking about what he did." Often I find this is punishment enough, but if it isn't, I'm rarely too harsh when I've let MY angry moment pass.
Jenny Schroeder, LaCrosse, WI

forum parents forum

I try my best to label my emotions and the reasons for them. When my anger is intense, the child goes into his bedroom for a few minutes so both can cool down. Refrain always from the physical—it NEVER "fits the crime!"

Mary Mumma, Detroit, MI

Brian (3) is always given the ground rules and one warning. If behavior continues, he's sent to SIT, not PLAY, in his bedroom. When he and I are ready to have him come out, I talk to him and he tells me what he did wrong and what he'll do next time. He's never been in his room more than 10 minutes. He receives one swat from the paddle if the behavior was to cause harm to himself or others.

Gayle Baker, Greeley, CO

"Just Wait Till You Have Children of Your Own!"

"Most people approach parenthood with expectations about the kind of disciplinarian they are going to be. They themselves have been disciplined, and long ago may have sworn to themselves that they're never going to 'hurt' the child, or 'be mean,' 'be unreasonable.'

Furthermore, before they had children of their own, they have been confronted in public places with parents punishing children . . . . They have seen parents with a stranglehold on children's arms, dragging them down the street. They have seen parents insult and threaten children at restaurants or wheel them wailing through supermarkets . . .

Then, as their children grow, many people find themselves transported back to the scenes they played as children or that they have viewed played out by other parents and children . . . . The aggression of children can transport parents back to childhood . . . . Unceasing tears, screams, slaps or childish logic can stir up a long ago childhood response—parents can feel like screaming or hitting back . . . .

The aggression of children can unleash powerful aggressive feelings in adults, and with these feelings, for some, an image of themselves comes crumbling down.

From the chapter "Authority Stage," in Ellen Galinsky's fascinating book of "passages" on parenting, BETWEEN GENERATIONS: THE SIX STAGES OF PARENTHOOD (Times Books, $15.95).

When my husband was a boy, he was chasing his brother and cracking his new bull whip. One crack hit the ceiling and ruined a new acoustical tile. His father made him cut up his whip into quarter-inch pieces. Believe me, he never did anything like that again and he vividly remembers it to this day. I wish I could be as inventive.

Ella Beth Goetschuis, Houston, TX

I work at a preschool with 2- to 6-year-olds and follow these procedures: 1) I set the child down until we're both ready to talk (gives us both a chance to cool off and become more objective). 2) I ask WHY the child did it to get a better perspective on the seriousness of the act. 3) WE talk about WHY the behavior was wrong, often by having the child put himself or herself in another's place ("How would you feel if someone took your lunch?"). I get the child to right the wrong, in order to learn to accept responsibility for his or her own actions. 5) WE talk about how the child can prevent that behavior in the future.

Jan Handley, Goleta, CA

When my 4-year-old labeled his furniture "bed," "wall," and so on with crayon scribbles, the best punishment was to calmly hand HIM cleanser and a sponge. His crayons were taken away for a week, too.

Laraine Worby, Holliston, MA

When my son soaked the kitchen with the spray attachment at the sink, his punishment was a fast lesson in drying things off. It took a long time, but he's much more careful now.

Terry Porter, Carrollton, TX

As much as possible, I try to follow the advice of Rudolf Dreikers in his CHILDREN THE CHALLENGE. It's based on logical consequences. For example, if a child is called to dinner and doesn't come until it's cold, he either eats it cold or gets nothing at all. The key is to be consistent and to think what would happen if you weren't there to intervene—then let it happen, unless, of course, it's life threatening.

Mary Ellen Cooper, Glendale, AZ

In your search for disciplinary techniques that work, don't overlook one of the best sources of information you have to draw from—the children themselves.

How To Act After Being Sent to Your Room

Slam the door.
"I hate them!
"I hate them I hate them I hate them I hate them. I wish their heads would fall off! I wish they would get run over by a truck and never get up! This is my parents!"—grab doll, pull its head sideways, smash it to the ground. Kick it. "I'll get them and they'll be sorry."

Throw yourself on the bed diagonally—legs dangling off, head buried in pillow. "I get blamed for everything! Every single thing that happens in this creepy house is my fault! It's not fair! Me! Always me! What did I do to deserve this? Nothing! Did I ask to be born? Did I ask them to have me? Did I? I hate being the oldest! I hate it I hate it I hate it! The oldest always gets it—that's the story of my life!

"Oh who cares anyway. I wanted to go to my room. I'm glad I'm here. That's where I wanted to be."

Pick up the cat and hold it on your lap. Hug it. Lean over and rub your hair in its fur. "I love you. I love you so much. I love you, silly cat, cute cat, pretty cat. I love you and not anybody else. I love you I love you I love you I love you I love you. You're the only one in the family that I love. You're the only one who understands me." Hug it tighter.

"Nobody else understands me. Nobody. Everybody else is against me. Everyone but you. My mother doesn't care about me. She really doesn't—I know. She doesn't love me. She doesn't listen to me. I tried to tell her. I tried to explain, but does she care? She never wants to hear my side. Never! It's always her side. Her side's the right side; her side's the one! Anyone else's side? for-get it! She thinks she knows everything. Well, she doesn't! I hate her—BIG UGLY KNOW-IT-ALL. FATHEAD. JERK. I always get blamed! I always get picked on! I always get it! It's not fair!

"Just wait. Just wait—they'll regret it! I'm never ever ever ever speaking to them again as long as I ever live—even if they speak to me first, even if they beg me. Just let them try. They'll see. I've had it. I'll give them the silent treatment for the rest of their lives.

"Boy if I die will they be sorry."

Open the door and stand at the top of the stairs. Yell, "Can I come down yet?"

From HOW TO EAT LIKE A CHILD, by Delia Ephron. Copyright© 1977, 1978 by Delia Ephron. Reprinted by permission of Viking Penguin Inc.

parents forum paren

Q The best and the worst of

My daughters (6 and 8) had teddy bear picnics. Each child brought her favorite bear, and ribbons were awarded for the biggest, oldest, softest, etc. Refreshments included teddy bear cookies for each guest to decorate. Games can include teddy tag, ring around the teddy, etc. They were the best parties we ever had.

Kathy Hermes Overland Park, KS

My daughter (5) loves having a treasure hunt. We make up clues incorporating the party theme and, finally, tell where to look for the next clue. Hidden with each clue is a present for one guest. At the end of the hunt, each child has a present and we are ready for cake and ice cream!

Claudia Tolar Running Springs, CA

A local community center holds theme parties for kids. The children do artwork, plays, or other imaginative activities. Themes include pirates, circus world, space fantasy, etc.

Shirley Cohn Burnaby, BC

Take an instant picture of each child to take home.

Maryann Shutan Highland Park, IL

At 3 my son had his party at a ranch. We had one hour of corral riding (the adults walked the horses) and an hour-long hayride for adults and children. The kids enjoyed all the farm animals.

One neighbor rented a dance studio with instructor to teach break dancing to 12-year-olds.

Donna Cianciulli Miami, FL

For my son's third birthday, I bought a pinata from a party shop and filled it with goodies (sugarless gum and healthy snacks). We hung it outside and everyone took turns giving it a whack with a broom handle. The pinata was so hard to break that even I had a hard time, but no one seemed to mind. It took up a lot of time, showed everyone how to take turns, and had a fun surprise at the end.

Debbie Parnakian Huntington Beach, CA

As the children arrive, they take a seat around a large sheet of white paper. Each child designs a section and it can be cut up and sent home with each child. You can have a theme, but it's not necessary.

Linda Merry St. Louis Park, MN

When we play games, there is no winner. Everyone gets a prize for playing. We like "fishing" (throwing a play fishing pole over into a pretend river to catch a small toy or prize).

Vicki Piipo Richland, WA

For my 7-year-old's party I laminated posterboard squares which we sewed together into sticker books and decorated with inexpensive stickers. It made a good party favor that the kids assembled themselves.

Sharon Amastae El Paso, TX

Before the party, put a scoop of ice cream in paper-foil cupcake liners and keep them in the freezer until ready to serve.

Ann Miranda Fullerton, CA

We had a party for our 4-year-old in the gym of our local park. The kids brought trikes/bikes to ride while the parents rested between activities.

Karen Burkland Sherman Oaks, CA

Do an art project, such as rock painting or string art (dip string in poster paint and lay across large pieces of art paper). I still think charades is the best party game ever. Have a lot of ideas ready; the kids never seem to want to quit.

Marcia Len Cohoes, NY

Set the table with plain white paper plates and cups. Set a box of felt pens or crayons in the center and have the children decorate their own. This will entertain them while they're waiting for the food.

Lori Stefanishion Drumheller, Alberta

For older children, play "unwrap the package." Wrap a small favor in several layers of different wrapping paper. The children sit in a circle and pass the package around as music plays. When the music stops, the child holding the package unwraps one layer. The child who removes the last layer gets to keep the favor.

Barbara Deleebeeck Stavanger, Norway

For our 6-year-old, we had ice cream with all kinds of toppings. The kids could make banana splits or sundaes or just have it plain.

Loree Jurek Seminole, TX

Give Play-Doh for gifts and have the kids make an animal, monster, or whatever. Give a prize for the best sculpture.

Cynthia Wagner Montebello, CA

For my son's sixth birthday I made castle pieces (cones, towers, and turrets) from grey construction paper and had the children make castles using a dish of glue and a brush. It kept them busy and when they were finished, I lined the castles up in the middle of the table so they could be admired while the cake was being served.

Pat Brinkmann Palo Alto, CA

Vicki Lansky's Practical Parenting

BIRTHDAY PARTIES

Tips, recipes, decorating ideas, games, songs, planning sheets and more.

forum parents forum

. . birthday parties!

My son's first birthday party was a classic example of my over-enthusiasm and unrealistic expectations. I invited every child in the neighborhood! All the older kids descended on the cake and ice cream and favors and then disappeared. The ones who were left tore through the presents at the speed of light!

Georgia Walsh Alexandria, VA

The worst was for a 4-year-old, attended by two children and ten adult relatives. All I heard was "Quiet down. Don't be so noisy." It wasn't even fun for me!

Kathy Hickok Delray Beach, FL

All of the worst birthday parties were held at McDonald's and Burger King where the children are supposed to behave and sit still. Both of my children prefer parties in people's houses, with not too many children. The best one was held outside.

Harriet Landry Belford, NJ

Evening parties seem to be the worst. Kids are too tired.   *Unsigned*

The worst birthday parties I've given and attended were for children under 4. They're too young to appreciate being the honored one or being a guest. As hosts, they want to win all the games and keep all the prizes. As guests, they want to keep the presents for themselves. Parents tend to invite too many children for too many hours. The rule I follow is from FEED ME! I'M YOURS: "the number of guests should not exceed the number of years of your child's age." This works!

Karen Gromada Cincinnati, OH

The worst party was one for 3-year-olds at a pizza place. The children were terrified of the people dressed in animal costumes and clung to their moms.

Karen Dockrey Burke, VA

The worst party my girls attended was at a roller rink. It was so noisy we all had headaches when we left.

Mary Ellen Cooper Glendale, AZ

The worst party included a viewing of THE EMPIRE STRIKES BACK on a VCR. It was mayhem!

Myra Weaver Hollywood, FL

I once made the mistake of inviting the mothers as well as the kids. I had a simple lunch planned for the children and an elaborate one for the mothers (buffet style). There was no way I could keep both groups happy.

Linda Phelps Clarendon Hills, PA

The worst was a party at McDonald's. The noise and confusion were awful. The birthday child seemed to get lost in the shuffle. And all this was topped off by poor food. YUCK!

Judi Hoey Morristown, NJ

The VERY worst was the one I had for my 6-year-old (obviously my first child) to which we invited her entire first-grade class of 32. Pandemonium, with all scheduled games played in half the time allotted, kids fighting all over the house, and screaming you wouldn't believe.

Kathryn Ring Scottsdale, AZ

For my daughter's eighth birthday we had a slumber party. One of the guests had several slices of pizza and two pieces of birthday cake. During the night she threw up all over my sleeping bag and insisted on having her parents pick her up at 2:30 a.m. Definitely not a fun party!

Kathi Baldwin Rancho Cucamongo, CA

It's still too painful to think about. I'll tell you in another five years when I get over it.

Connie Tenn West Linn, OR

Miss Manners on Birthday Parties

America's foremost—and funniest—authority on etiquette, Judith Martin, has written a primer for everyone worried about the future of civilization: Miss Manners' Guide to Rearing Perfect Children *(Atheneum, 1984, $19.95). A complete guide to civilizing children from birth to marriage, it covers just about every social situation imaginable. For those who bemoan less-than-perfect results in their child-rearing efforts, Miss Manners offers these words of comfort: "Stages are what we call the unbearable things children think of to do while waiting for child-rearing to take effect." And she stresses the last rule of child-rearing: "Never give up."*

Here is a sampling of Miss Manners on children's birthday parties.

* * * *

Most children Miss Manners knows give parties at least once a year.

Presumably, they do it to get presents.

Even aside from greed, however, children need to give and attend birthday parties because these horrible events teach them civilized social behavior, although not always so's you'd recognize it. The principle of community fun through the performance of individual duty and the restraint of unacceptable urges is a difficult one to grasp, and a great many people go through life without getting very good at it.

Then comes the necessity of learning to disguise greed. An astute child may understand why it is necessary to perform the courtesy of saying "hello" to someone who has not yet handed over his offering, but the need for social niceties once the present has changed hands may not be so clear. Many rehearsals are necessary to perfect the unnatural technique of seeming surprised and pleased at each and every present, no matter how paltry, redundant, and unappealing. A list of stock remarks—such as "That doesn't matter, I wanted another one" and "Wow!"—is handy, along with instructions in the appropriate facial expressions.

The toughest test of all is the concept that the birthday child should probably not win the games, but certainly must not, even if he does win, go off with the prizes. Some people cannot bring themselves to impose this standard, running the risk that their children will grow up to take home Caribbean vacation tickets and new cars from the charity balls of which they are the chairmen.

parents forum parent

Q How do you make good food

Sprinkle cinnamon on applesauce and brown rice, dribble honey on brown rice and steamed vegetables. Make faces in their oatmeal with sunflower seeds, raisins, or nuts.

M. Schultz   Rancho Palos Verdes, CA

When I serve spinach, my husband and daughter have a wrestling match after dinner. Of course, they eat a lot of spinach first because they both want to be strong enough to win.

Claudia Tolar   Running Springs, CA

No matter what clever tricks I try, they always want to know "what's in it?" and if it's not on the current list of non-gaggables, forget it!

Cynthia Carlton   Los Angeles, CA

Use it as a reward instead of candy. "If you do such and such, you can have an apple (or a carrot, or whatever)." Cook breads that have carrots, pumpkin, zucchini, etc.

Jan Keating   River Forest, IL

I follow a Latin American proverb that translates loosely to: "To a hungry man there is no bad bread." If my child says he's hungry, he can choose from two or three wholesome alternatives. If he won't accept any of them, I assume he's just not hungry enough.

Susan Roberts   Jackson, MS

Our son enjoys cutting his own cheese and hard-boiled eggs with a cheese slicer.

Susan Sherwin   Union, NE

Banana with peanut butter is a hit at our house. So are apple slices and raisins made into faces, and cooked vegetables (broccoli and cauliflower) pureed with cheese in a blender.

Suzette Kirby   Sioux Falls, SD

I introduced vegetables before fruits and other sweet foods so my child got used to the taste before getting turned on to sweets. I also gave her whole grains before refined grains. I vary the texture and color of the foods at each meal so they're visually appealing and interesting. Her dad and I say "yum yum," smack our lips, etc., when we eat or feed her nutritious foods. If she doesn't like something, we don't make a big deal of it, and try again later.

Janese Woodville   Eureka, CA

Use your imagination. Hot cereal becomes "porridge" like the three bears eat. Raisins and nuts make great eyes and noses on a variety of foods, and food coloring does wonders.

Donna Cianciulli   Miami, FL

I add cinnamon to bland vegetables like carrots and squash. I sneak dried milk and wheat germ into casseroles. I serve two vegetables every night so they can choose. We renamed some foods (broccoli = trees).

Cam Wilsie   Clio, MI

Good—But Not So Good—For You

Q: *I'm writing to beg you to consult with some more pediatricians. In FEED ME, I'M YOURS you recommend that carrot sticks not be given to children under 12-18 months—but on the next page you recommend them for babies over one year. All the doctors I have talked with do NOT recommend raw carrots, celery or apple pieces for children under 5 years, or nuts for children under 7 years. Why not recommend that these hard foods always be grated or cooked? You would be doing a service to warn parents not to serve these common and dangerous foods.*

JoeLynn Keniston   Aloha, OR

A: I called several local pediatricians with this question about foods which cause choking. Each had different foods he/she was concerned about, and different age recommendations for those foods. But I found out other interesting information. Gagging and choking, which may cause the aspiration of foods into the lungs, are different from choking to death because of blocked air passages.

Hot dogs and grapes have been causes of DEATH. Their real danger lies in their cylindrical shape, and one solution is to cut them lengthwise, turn and cut again, so that they are no longer a perfect plug for the air passages. Popcorn and nuts are best avoided before ages 3-4, because they can cause choking, although they rarely cause death. Carrots and other hard fruits and vegetables pose the same problem, and solutions include the ones you suggest.

I have added hot dogs to the list of foods not recommended for young children in the this edition of FEED ME, I'M YOURS, since they are a leading cause of choking in children. I'm struggling with what to do about the items you mention. I think your doctors' recommendation of 5 and 7 years as the age limit for introducing children to small, hard foods may cover the doctors' feelings of responsibility—but I don't think it's humanly possible to abide by it. What you may not serve at home a child is bound to come across somewhere else after the age of three.

Vicki

forum parents forum

appeal to your kids?

I introduce new foods to them at lunch, *without* Dad! I eat them. I let my daughter help prepare the food if possible while I explain how it will help our bodies grow and stay healthy.
Paula Hall   Bonners Ferry, ID

I told my son there was a secret suprise inside his hard-boiled egg. Now he loves eggs, and he's a very fussy eater.
Karen Cook   San Ramon, CA

I disguise green beans or carrots by mixing them in with rice, potatoes, and macaroni, which they love. I also limit snacking so they are definitely hungry at mealtime and will eat almost anything with no problem.
Janet Bauer   Islip Terrace, NY

It's amazing how appealing nutritious food is when there is no junk food around!
Jill Heasley   Fresno, CA

Cut cheese with an animal-shaped cookie cutter and give it a raisin face. My kids will eat almost anything off those compartment-type trays, too.
Pat Spiker   Columbus, OH

I always steam vegetables. They retain their bright color and firm texture. It really makes a difference.
Cheryl Kronberger   Oak Park, MI

I lie and cheat! I hide zucchini in muffins, say that small shrimp is chicken, call milk "grouch juice," and give them a multiple vitamin every day.
Kris Gialdini   Fremont, CA

My best hint to encourage protein consumption is to coat the inside of an ice cream cone with a thin layer of baby food meat. Toddlers think of it as a special treat.
Cindy Coppage   W. Hartford, CT

My daughter refuses to drink milk, so I put it in just about everything I cook.
Ellen Hodgins   Nipawin, Sask.

I make a lot of salads. The different colors and textures really appeal to my daughter. Spaghetti, lasagna, and chili have universal appeal to children and are also very nutritious.
Birgit Willigar   Miami, FL

My husband and I joyously eat our greens, giving abundant compliments to the chef. I've never been so healthy or eaten so many vegetables in my life, but we haven't fooled any kids yet.
Unsigned

I have a special lunch box in the refrigerator for healthy snacks. My daughter loves serving herself.
Kathy Lord   Rochester, MN

I give my daughter a choice of two or three vegetables for dinner. To get her to eat eggs, I ask, "Do you want butter or salt on them?" She always says, "Butter *and* salt." Kids love to have choices and feel in control.
M. E. Genovesi   Lake Ronkonkoma, NY

I cut tofu slices with a cookie cutter. Maybe it's gruesome, but my daughter loves to "bite the kitty-cat's toes off," etc.!
Michele Price   Alexandria, VA

I've served only nutritious foods from the start. Our children (3 and 5) don't know about junk food yet. They aren't picky eaters, and I think it's because sugar and salt aren't ruling their appetites.
Jennifer Dawson   Shushan, NY

My 5-year-old enjoys a platter of cold finger foods: apples, bananas, turkey sticks, olives, etc.
Lisa Smith   Hurst, TX

When I make pancakes, I always put in wheat germ, and sometimes bananas. When I serve something new, I give them a tiny bit. Quite often they surprise themselves and like it. They usually eat vegatables that are stir-fried. Some things they'll eat if they're mixed with something else, like milk on cereal, eggs in egg salad, etc. I try to explain nutrition in terms they understand: good food will help them run faster and ride bikes longer.
Harriet Landry   Belford, NJ

Let them use party toothpicks with colored frills to pick up carrot circles, cheese cubes, little meatballs, etc.
Unsigned

I have very little success in this arena. I consider myself lucky if my son eats *at all!* I often stand his sandwich quarters on end and call them sailboats. Another trick is to let them eat hot dog pieces (I know, a deadly product) with toothpicks, *with supervision.* We even make hot dog bunnies with frilly toothpicks. My husband makes up silly names for foods like "Mickey Mouse Stew," which often works.
Randi Steeves   Hamden, CT

Put sugar on it!
Robbie Fulmer (age 11)   Ann Arbor, MI

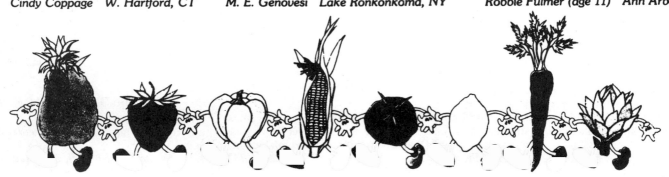

parents forum paren

Q How have you coped with the worst "gross habit" your child has had?

Our Sheldon never had a pacifier... We didn't want him to learn any bad habits.

from Do They Ever Grow Up by Lynn Johnston (Meadowbrook Press)

My 2-year-old spits out anything that he takes a dislike to, no matter where we are. I wish I knew how to get him to stop!
Cathy Kienzle, Bow Island, Alta.

My 4-year-old tends to "hold herself" or scratch in "private places." I think this may be due in part to her late potty training; she still can't get over not wearing a diaper. I guess I'm not alone—when we're in public and I ask her to stop I often see other parents smiling understandingly.
Barbara Sattora, Rush, NY

My 5-year-old used to widen his eyes, drop his jaw and make his mouth into the very smallest "O" possible. It looked as if he were clearing his sinuses or popping his ears. We ignored it for a week, then mentioned that it looked very strange. He stopped.
Kathy Hickok, Delray Beach, FL

At 23 months our sweet little cherub delighted in doing a B.M. and then pulling out a fistful to show anyone who was nearby. At the time I was studying Rudolf Dreikurs' CHILDREN: THE CHALLENGE for a graduate course. According to the book, adults need to determine the goal behind a child's misbehavior. Is the child seeking attention (most common), power or revenge, or showing inadequacy? Our daughter loved the attention she received when Mom and Dad looked horrified and rushed her off to the bathroom. I realized what was happening when, after our reaction, she smiled. Solution: We extinguished her behavior in one day by NOT reacting either verbally or nonverbally.
Julie Melville, Clovis, CA

LOUD sniffling and great big juicy sneezes without a tissue. As my child is allergic to housedust, when it's really bad, I medicate, but I'd prefer not to.
Unsigned

Spitting! His daddy chews tobacco on occasion and my son learned quickly. When he forgot and spit in the living room, we made it a rule to spit only when "working" outside.
Donna Holmes, Perry, OH

My niece (age 2) sucks her thumb with one hand while she tucks her other hand down the front of her diaper. THEN she switches hands!
Linda Neslund, Kingston, NY

Masturbation, which usually proved most embarrassing for the "observer." We simply said that was an "in your own room" activity.
Peggy Nelson, Deephaven, MN

I point it out to my child when we see someone else doing something that "doesn't look very nice." It helps.
Lori Stefanishion, Drumheller, Alta.

My son pokes and fondles his belly-button. Bib-front overalls help him be more discreet.
Carrie Bezak, Highland Park, MI

I was thrilled when my son finally became potty trained, but I found that there are some drawbacks. When we're at the pool, if he has to go he simply pulls his pants down and does so. At least he finds an out-of-the-way place.
Tammy Carroll, Anaheim, CA

Stephanie picks her nose and eats it, a charming habit she learned from our neighborhood "Ralphie" (PP column, July-Aug., '82). Our pediatrician noticed the inflamed condition of her nostrils and asked if she was a nose picker. I confessed that she was and he advised applying Neosporin ointment. Now when her nose becomes sore she gets the ointment and applies it herself. It doesn't work to tell her her habit makes me sick to my stomach. I have also told her I will make a sign for her: "Hi, I'm Stephanie, and I pick my nose." This usually makes her stop for the moment.
Kathi Baldwin, Rancho Cucamonga, CA

At 18 months, it's food throwing. We praise her a lot for handing us the food first and clean her up and remove her from the highchair as soon as she's through eating. We also tell her NO. At this point, she'll say, "No," to herself. We know "this, too, shall pass."
Karen Dockery, Columbus, IN

My children have all done everything. I wrote you once for help in stopping my then 3-year-old from putting her blanket in her nose. I thought she'd stopped when her friend was repulsed by it. I just found out that she's been sneaking the habit at night for the last two years.
Jerri Oyama, Northridge, CA

Sorry, I'd rather not say until I hear of one to top it!
Jeannine Imhoff, Cincinnati, OH

forum parents forum

Q What food jags have your kids taken up, and how have you reacted?

Bean burritos and kielbasa and frosted flakes, for six months. I've just lectured, which has not helped.

Mary McDonald, Chardon, OH

Colored milk with the cereal—orange, blue, whatever. I let my son have it but switched to natural food colors, hoping they're better for him. The acute phase lasted six months. The only ill effect has been the dentist's thinking he was taking medication because his tongue was orange.

Mrs. G. Marshall, Fremont, CA

My 18-month-old just went through a food jag during which he would eat only peanut-butter and cheese. It lasted two months—a lot longer than the books say jags last. I was frustrated, but since he appeared healthy and energetic, I didn't worry too much.

Connie Oliphint, Overton, TX

At about 16 months Jess ate almost nothing but bananas, up to six a day. Of course I worried and tried to tempt her with a more balanced diet, but I was grateful to have her binge on bananas rather than junk food. It lasted about a month; no ill effects.

Judith Hoey, Morristown, NJ

Liverwurst sandwiches for breakfast! I'm just thankful it's that and not "sugar coated chocolate zinger cereal."

Unsigned

Spaghetti-Os, for the last eight months. We try playing airplane and use reverse psychology, but sometimes nothing works.

Mrs. S. Thompson, Kansas City, MO

Sarah seems to be systematically eliminating many of the healthy foods I used to count on her to eat. "I don't like it any more" now applies to yogurt, cottage cheese, and American cheese. She could exist on macaroni and cheese and tuna fish. There is NOTHING we can do. She's very pleasant, but very firm.

Lenie Bershad, Southfield, MI

Yogurt, yogurt and yogurt—only peach. I did nothing for about two weeks and my son finally decided he wanted some of the baby's food. After three months, yogurt's still what he wants most. Okay, I don't have to cook so much. I'm sure one day he'll get over it.

Kyle Lutz, Mill Valley, CA

For two months it was Dannon yogurt and cheeseburgers. I kept my mouth shut and quit offering any variety. He soon began to ask for "something different."

Carrie Bezak, Highland Park, MI

At eight months to a year, my baby would have been happy to eat nothing but puffed wheat. I would put a few puffs on other foods, which she would then eat readily.

Lori Stefanishion, Drumheller, Alta.

CHEERIOS. The kid lived on them (Honey Nut variety, I confess with shame) for nine months, between ages 1 and 2. It eased up when she could finally chew fresh fruits and vegetables.

Belinda Stanley, Conroe, TX

Our 3-year-old would live on peanut butter and honey sandwiches, if we allowed it. We're fairly flexible with breakfast and lunch,

but he can have peanut butter sandwiches at only one meal. At dinner time, he must eat what the rest of the family has.

Becky Gammons, Beaverton, OR

We have exposed our son to such a wide range of foods that his jags now will be a week of cheese, berries and bananas; a week of meat, meat, meat; a week of peas at every meal, then corn on the cob. He'll eat eggs for five straight days, then not touch them for a month.

Maureen Morriston, Ft. Mitchell, KY

My 2-year-old just wanted olives to eat for five days. He even woke up in the middle of the night once and was into them in the refrigerator.

Mrs. R. Reese, Canoga Park, CA

At 30, I'm still on a food jag. I'll eat only apricot jelly sandwiches for lunch, and if I could get away with it, I'd cook breakfast three times a day. I drove my mother crazy. What is this big deal about food, anyway?

Karen Leitch, Calgary, Alta.

Cinnamon graham crackers, for about six months, followed shortly by ice cream and peanut M & Ms (the latter thanks to Grandma), which we are still into.

Tammy Carroll, Anaheim, CA

At one time Ryan ate only scrambled eggs, bananas and hotdogs for about a year. I switched to chicken and turkey hotdogs for better nutrition but didn't press him otherwise. Now he will have nothing to do with eggs and bananas and eats only an occasional hotdog.

Kathi Baldwin, Rancho Cucamonga, CA

A Glossary of Kitchen Terms
from *The Taming of the CANDY Monster,*

Bananas	tropical disease which affects a parent as a child swings into 6th month of a food jag
Jelly Bean	the only "vegetable" all kids will eat
Peanut Butter	staff of life

Too Much Variety

After observing the limited kinds of food available in villages in Asia and Africa (limited particularly during certain seasons), I sometimes wonder if the eating behavior our children sometimes demonstrate is a result of our offering too much variety. We also structure eating times. A study from the University of Iowa has indicated that children left to their own eating times will eat six times a day. In rural or tropical areas, children may have access to fruits, vegetables, nuts, etc., which makes snacking easy and routine. I was troubled by my children's rejection of my offerings. We have come to accept the fact that Anne doesn't like onions and Joy doesn't like oatmeal. We continue to dislike the idea of wasting food. Cabbage is currently in again for some of the children. And I keep telling myself that if the food available in the house provides good nutrition, the children will be well fed.

From RAISING HAPPY HEALTHY CHILDREN, by Karen Olness, M.D.

parentsforum

Q How have you prepared an older child for a new baby?

Among other things, I took a tour of the labor, delivery and postpartum floor with our daughter. She was awed, but it was helpful to her when she came to visit me and the new baby in the hospital. I also planned a birthday party for the new baby when we came home, and everybody got a present.

No Name Included

If my daughter wanted something when I was busy with the baby, I'd say, "My hands are busy right now." It didn't sound so personal, and it pacified her until I was free.

Carol Taylor, Birmingham, AL

I have three points of advice. First, don't worry yourself sick over the transition for children at home. I drained myself mentally the first few days, then realized that I was the one having the rough time adjusting. I always wanted to be saying and doing the right things—and no mom is perfect. Second, feel successful about your busy days if you have spent a little special time with each child. You've done well if you've found time to give each child his or her own hugs and kisses and personal comments. Third, say YES to whatever help a friend offers you. Enjoy being pampered—you deserve it.

Vickie Poucher, Kalamazoo, MI

I took our 2½-year-old with me to the doctor every month. He heard the baby's heartbeat and my questions, talked to the doctor and nurses. He enjoyed being in on things and reporting home to Daddy, and I enjoyed his company. Afterward, don't be overprotective. Hovering over the baby with too many restrictions only suggests inappropriate behavior. We let our son experiment, within reason, and learn for himself what his sister did and didn't like.

Jodi Junge, Huntingdon Valley, PA

Always tell an older child well before; do any moving, rearranging or changing of furniture "because you're bigger," not "to make room for baby," and do it all months ahead of time. No syrupy stories about a new baby to play with, but frankness—babies cry a lot and don't do much for several months. To you, baby is a joy and a blessing, but not to very many 3-year-olds!

Lea Moran, Cortland, OH

We feel the most important help our older child had was a good three years of our attention before she had a sibling. This got her off to a good start and almost eliminated any rivalry problems we might have had.

Candace Waldrum, Paris, TX

> If you want to understand how your two-year-old feels about the new baby, imagine your husband, after two years of wedded bliss, saying, "I have a nice surprise for you! I'm bringing home a new wife so you'll have a playmate!"

I gave my 2-year-old nephew a T-shirt that says, "I'm the BIG BROTHER," right before his sister was born. He wore it to visit his mom in the hospital and on trips to the pediatrician.

Barbara Evans, Stone Mountain, GA

Each of our children was 3 when the next came along. We moved each to a twin bed a few months before the due date, stressing it was because he or she was so grown up now. Later we asked if it would be all right for us to let the baby use the crib, since the big kids didn't need it. No problems. It never hurts to remind the older ones that they were cuddled as much and fussed over, too. Pull out baby pictures to prove it!

Beverley Spindler, Roseville, MI

When our last child was on the way, our girls were 7 and 8. I bought two very good books with lots of pictures explaining the how and whys of birth. They loved seeing how "their" baby was developing. It was always "our" baby, and they were as excited as my husband and I were. It's been three years now, and the poor "baby" has had three mothers from day one—he can't get away with much!

Susan Lipke, Harrietta, MI

We prepared our 22-month-old by exposing him to as many new babies as possible prior to the arrival of his sister. As a consequence, he wasn't upset at all—she was just another baby. We make sure to give him the attention he needs, when he needs it. No problems so far, except for needing a few extra arms sometimes.

Mary Lou England, Natchez, MS

We showed our child pictures of intrauterine development, such as are found in the book BIRTH OF A BABY and took him to childbirth films. He saw a sex education special on the PBS station. If we had it to do over, we would NOT prepare him so well. We put too much emphasis in the new baby, and he reacted.

Dana Clark, Santa Barbara, CA

My son, then 2½, didn't really understand what was about to happen even though it was carefully explained. On the way out of the hospital HE was in my lap in the wheelchair and the new baby was held by the nurse —not Mommy OR Daddy. We're now expecting our third. The children have been asking for a new baby—but that won't make any difference. Jealousy is inevitable no matter how well the sibling is prepared.

Jerri Oyama, Northridge, CA

In retrospect, I found that it was I who should have been better prepared. I perpetuated Brian's aggressive responses (hitting, ripping, breaking toys) by my own extreme concern for his hurt feelings. He sensed my sympathy and tested me beyond what was called for. I was so worried about him that I went so far as not to snuggle the baby when he was around.

Wendy Short, Bethel Park, PA

A BABY IS AN ANGEL WHOSE WINGS DECREASE AS HIS LEGS INCREASE

parents forum

Q How do you teach a toddler to play with an infant?

Are you kidding!? I've a 6½-month-old girls and an (almost) 2-year-old girl, and I can hardly pry the two of them apart! They're inseparable. I wouldn't have it any other way. I hope they stay this close.
Donna Schreier, St. Paul, MN

I always explain about "big" boys and girls. They are bigger and older and can do so many more things. Babies learn by watching *them*. All my toddlers do real well and *act* like "Mommies" and "Daddies."
Rose Arndt Kusturin, Knox, IN

We tell Jordan not to hit Bryan, because Bryan is a tiny baby and tiny babies get hurt very easily. Besides we stress the fact that when he was a tiny baby no one hurt him.
W. Lyles, Aurora, CO

Supervise a period of "play together" each day, show by example, have plenty of discussions with the toddler, use the cat and/or dog to practice on, then say lots of prayers that the youngest will live to see her first birthday.
Mrs. Pi Johnston, Hartsdale, NY

You *don't*! Say "Be careful!" or "No!" We say "Gentle" softly with babies, plants, books, and special things and then *show* what gentle means. He walked on only one baby, showing her how much he loved her.
Kris Gialdini, Fremont, CA

I showed my soon-to-be 3-year-old daughter things to do with her new baby brother (patting gently on back, making soft toys bounce for him, smiling, doing tricks for him from a safe distance away). Big sister loved to bring diapers for Mom to change baby.
Bonnie Erwinloomis, Austin, TX

I try to show them ways to play. They are not allowed to hold the baby unless I am there. Usually, I put the baby in a car seat (which I use as an infant seat) and have them show him rattles and other toys.
Mrs. T. G. Stanton, Mendota Heights, MN

Parents teach in the toughest school in the world—the school for people making.

We have been fairly successful here. We practiced being "gentle" with the dog before the birth. When my older is angry, we tell him it's okay to hit the floor or the punching bag. After all, he has to express anger somehow.
Nancy Wrathen, Los Angeles, CA

I play *with* our 2½-year-old and 5-month-old, together—letting the older one hold her, clap her hands, give her a rattle, and so forth. If I'm not there to monitor what happens, the older one will pull the baby's arms to sit her up. Then, of course, the baby falls back crying.
S. Laughlin, Cincinnati, OH

I encouraged Chad (3 years old) to hold his younger sister, talk, and hold rattles for her within our supervision—but never totally trusted him. Once I walked through the room where the baby was playing quietly on a blanket and saw our son pounding contentedly with a hammer on a piece of wood. I hesitated and then thought, no, he wouldn't do anything, thought again—and took the baby with me.
Gail Schutz, White Hall, IL

Keep an eye on them until the "infant" can take care of himself (fight back or scream).
Lorna Overhold, Wind Gap, PA

I have just the opposite problem—my 3½-year-old girl *drags* her 9-month-old brother around by lifting him under the armpits and hoisting. We were careful when he was younger to explain to her that the baby could break just like some of her toys, but we also think it best to let her touch and hold.
Lorrie Winters, Renton, WA

It was very hard for my older one to see the baby as a live thing. He liked to sit on him. Once I heard the baby make a strange noise. I turned around to see my 2-year-old standing on my 2-month-old baby's stomach! No permanent harm was done, but I almost had a heart attack!
Becky Wilkins, Lubbock, TX

I always used a baby doll to practice on with them—or a stuffed toy. But when I had three under age 4 I'd put the baby in the playpen in an infant seat to keep the others out. No near disasters.
Marcia Len, Cohoes, NY

A friend explained that a toddler does not see a baby as a person but as a plaything—much like a toy. This helped at a recent mothers' meeting when my aggressive 17-month-old daughter kept trying to "hug" a 3-week-old baby. By remembering this advice, I could relax and see my daughter's point of view. So, instead of yelling at her, I just distracted (or interested) her with other "toys."
Margie Goodell, Toledo, OH

I don't know. I have to admit this is one area in which I failed miserably. I was so afraid of my 3-year-old hurting the baby, I discouraged togetherness. I wish I could have done it differently.
Linda Merry, St. Louis Park, MN

I had to wheel my newborn from room to room with me in a buggy in order to protect him from my 2-year-old. (You would have had to know my 2-year-old to under?stand why!)
Jill Heasley, Fresno, CA

Near disaster: A 2½-year-old neighbor child was picking up my 2-month-old off the floor by her hair. Then I called her mother. We decided she had just been trying to get the baby to sit by itself, like the little girl's 9-month-old brother did. She was probably as confused and upset by the baby's crying as I was. I had her over the next day, and let her sit on the sofa with the baby. I told her again never to pick the baby up by herself and why.

I have found one thing I never considered before: that not only do you have to anticipate your own child's actions, but those of all their friends who visit your home. It really wears me out.
Jeannine Imhoff, Cincinnati, OH

parents forum parent

Q At what age did you allow children to play outdoors alone?

Whether or not you allow your child to play out alone depends on where you live—on a farm or in the city, on a busy street or in a cul-de-sac—and on your child's personality. Some children seem to be more suited to going it "alone" than others. Not a small consideration is the temperament of the child next door and the children in the neighborhood in general.

Families with fenced yards and the safest of situations tend to begin to allow their children to go out alone when they are 2 to 2½ years old. Playing out alone "in front" or in an unfenced area is allowed for most kids from about 3½ to 5 years of age—salted with clear rules about boundaries (a painted line or a ladder across the bottom of the driveway) and stern admonishments about letting parents always know whereabouts. Those with older siblings to watch over them seem to have privileges a bit earlier.

Obviously, it's a problem for all parents, and some of the responses recount the horrors about which we all have nightmares occasionally.

I started by playing outdoors WITH my twins, making sure they knew where our yard boundaries are and not letting them go over them. When they were about 3, I let them play outside alone for 15 minutes to a half-hour, though I couldn't help standing by the window. I gradually increased their length of time outdoors and decreased the time I spent at the window. So far it has worked very well; the twins like to tattle on each other, so I always know who's doing what, and where! Now, at age 4, they're allowed to play on the sidewalk but are not allowed to go past the corners of the block (luckily it's a short block and I can see them if I glance out the window). I have explained that driveways can be as dangerous as the street, because cars back out and little children can't always be spotted.

Robyn Neuman, Beaver Dam, WI

Between 4 and 5, when they know their names, address and phone number. They are grounded at home for a day if they go somewhere without telling me first. I am over-cautious by some neighbors' standards, but there are too many sick people out there. My children are my responsibility, and they are young for a short time.

Jeannine Imhoff, Cincinnati, OH

At 4, Sarah began playing with the neighborhood children. Rules: she must tell her dad or me if she's leaving our yard, must tell us if she goes from one house to another. We live on a very quiet dead-end street and all the kids on the block cross the street themselves. At first I was very uncomfortable with this, but when every child but Sarah was allowed to do it, and she was left standing at the curb alone, we decided to loosen up. She's very bright and very careful about "looking both ways," so I try not to worry. HA!

Lenie Bershad, Southfield, MI

We are fortunate to live on one of the middle lots of a cul-de-sac with no traffic. Therefore, my 2¾-year-old is allowed to play out in front "unsupervised" (I'm looking out the window approximately every three minutes—no wonder I get more housework accomplished when she plays inside!).

Unsigned

It is different with each child. When I could leave Kate alone in a room in the house while I was in another room, I let her out in a fenced yard by herself. I made sure I removed all obvious things she could get hurt on.

J. Haynes, Albuquerque, NM

Together Outdoors

Do plan some outdoor activities together with your child. You may want to try some of the following activities:

Seeds. Plant some seeds, and watch them grow. Remember younger children are impatient for action, so select a seed variety that germinates quickly.

Shadows. Draw a shadow, and watch how it changes. Trace a shadow with a piece of chalk, and watch how the shadow changes during the day.

Wind. On a windy day, catch a bag of wind in a clear plastic bag. Ask your children what they see inside the bag.

Fly a kite. With young children a pinwheel is easier and more interesting, as it is closer and quicker to respond.

Lifestudy. Observe living things. Follow the path of an ant, find a worm, or catch a snail. Watch how an insect changes its path or climbs over an obstacle such as a small twig. Feed the birds. Have children note how different food attracts different birds.

I want to share an experience. One hot, sunny afternoon all the neighborhood children were playing outdoors and I was out doing yard work, as were my neighbors on both sides. The adults all went in, for various reasons, and the children decided to play across the street—all but one neighbors' son, Tommy, 3. He decided to jimmy a gate and climb the wall of his family's fourfoot pool to get his inner tube. Luckily, one neighbor happened to look out his back window in time to see just Tommy's fingers above the water. By the time he jumped his fence and dove in the pool, Tommy lay at the bottom. The boy's father and I had reached poolside by then. As we laid the child on the ground, we found no vital signs and he was blue. It took us almost two minutes to revive him. He has recovered 100 percent. We adults believe that NO MORE THAN five minutes passed from the time the last adult went inside and Tommy lay at the bottom of the pool.

I don't know if there is an answer or solution to supervising our children. I know they need their independence, but I also know how numb I felt after holding Tommy's lifeless body in my arms and praying for his cry as we administered first aid.

Thank you for letting me share.

Nedra O'Neill, Calumet Park, IL

I used to feel that our 3-year-old was safe in our quiet neighborhood when our faithful, attentive cocker spaniel was with her. The dog kept bullies in line and had even been known to "herd" the child from the street. Our habits changed dramatically the day they came home together and the dog dropped dead—strychnine, injected into a weiner, said the vet. If the child had seen the weiner first, she probably would have eaten it.

K. R., Scottsdale, AZ

forum parents forum

We have an open yard, with a lake just down the hill. I kept putting off the decision, but ran into problems when child #2 arrived. You can't keep a 3½-year-old locked up in the house forever, and with the new baby, we had to go out together when it fit into the baby's schedule. It frightened me, but I had to let her go. Every five minutes I was at the door looking and calling. After about a month I was able to send her out without really worrying every minute. We have set some rules: she is to stay within an imaginary boundary line, nothing is to go into the mouth (strange things can make you very sick), she is to check with me before going anywhere (even just beyond the boundary to get a lost toy) and she is to show herself at our picture window every so often so Mommy knows she's all right.

Mrs. R. Cradlin, Williamsburg, VA

I was so protective of my son that the older boys on the block teased him until I had to let him go. He was not allowed in the front yard alone until he was 4½ and not allowed to ride his bike in the street until 6½. I still cringe when he crosses the street, at 7—sometimes he doesn't watch for cars, though I lecture, threaten and tell him about items on careless children on TV and in the paper.

Jerri Oyama, Northridge, CA

Simple commands work best for us: "NOT ON THE ROAD," or "STAY ON THE DRIVEWAY!" These are lines a 2-year-old will parrot and hopefully remember.

Jodi Junge, Huntingdon Valley, PA

Our rules for children 4 and 2 are that if they're out of sight I want to know where they are and that they don't leave one area for another without asking first. If they break the rules or wander out of the declared "safe" zones, they are immediately brought inside (which actually punishes Mommy!).

Barbara Sattora, Rush, NY

Every year about 150,000 children in America are abducted. No responsible parent should allow a youngster to play alone. The children may be "ready," but so are the child kidnappers who are often also molesters and murderers. For more information about missing children, contact Missing Children Information Clearinghouse 1-800-342-0821.

Jane Anderson, Washington, DC

from *Do They Ever Grow Up* by Lynn Johnston (Meadowbrook Press)

Violence Plagues Sandbox

Hostilities erupted late today in the small, blue-and-white sandbox at the north corner of the E. H. Sandler backyard. Several witnesses observed Alyce Sandler, 3, and Cathy Washinsky, 4, bop each other on the heads with shovels in an attempt to uncover who had the red bucket first. Injuries were minor.

"She stole my bucket," accused Sandler. "I was using it first!"

Washinsky retorted, "It's *my* bucket! I brought it from home."

Gloria Sandler, mother of Alyce and part-owner of the sandbox, said, "I didn't actually see what happened, but these fights go on all the time lately. The girls don't seem to be able to play together for more than two minutes without a flare-up."

Carol Washinsky, mother of Cathy, advised, "The red bucket does belong to us,

but I really can't say who was using it at the time in question. I must add, though, that Alyce usually starts these fights. Don't quote me on that."

Following a cease fire, opposing sides have bivuoacked for the night in their respective camps. Peace talks are scheduled for the morning.

excerpted from *No More Tantrums* (Contemporary Books, 1987)

parentsforum

Q Will you share bedtime rituals and/or techniques?

Sometimes it seems that children from about 1 to 3 demand a great deal of attention at bedtime—including lots of HOLDING. They should be able to get to sleep without so much attention, we think, but they don't, and it's often years before they quietly put themselves to bed. Eventually they become a little more independent . . . and by then we're used to spending the time and even miss the ritual!

When my first child was born, my husband bought me a rocking recliner, and all three of us rocked and relaxed during our special time at night. As our family increased to four children, we felt this our best purchase ever. We still rock all four every night.
Gilda Henderson, Beeville, TX

Our 2-month-old goes to sleep without fussing if we hold him up against us so he can hear our heartbeats. Humming to him also makes him relax and soon fall asleep.
Brenda Merritt, Genoa, IL

When I'm relaxed, the baby (9 months) relaxes. I hold him for his bottle while he touches my face. After he's in the crib, I always return to his room and pick him up one more time. It comforts us both, and he usually goes to sleep easily.
Nikki Segall, Bloomington, MN

Our daughter has NEVER been on a schedule. At 1, I simply let her stay up 'til she gets tired (anywhere from 9:30 to 11 p.m.). A few minutes of rocking and she's sound asleep. I think not forcing a schedule on her makes her a happier, more contented child.
Sue Malley, Kalamazoo, MI

Our 2½-year-old loves to be chased upstairs by Mommy (or Daddy) "gorilla," complete with ape noises and heavy stepping. He laughs all the way up, but pretends to be afraid, seeking the safety of his crib. He climbs in and snuggles up to his well loved Raggedy Ann for protection. He's been conditioned to look at the clock—when the big hand points up, it's time for the Great Gorilla Chase to begin.
Sheri Sinykin, Madison, WI

We open up our hide-a-bed in the family room and our 2-year-old falls peacefully asleep between us while we watch TV at night. Then I put her to bed.
Barbara Yanez, Martinez, CA

I'm usually wiped out when naptime for my 2-year-old twins rolls around. I get myself a pillow and blanket and camp out on the floor (guarding the door so they can't get out). I leave the crib side down so they can get a toy if they want one, give them each a few books—and I crash. If they fuss, I have my standard line, "We're all resting now, we have our books. Let Mom sleep." If I'm not tired, I bring in a book to read, checkbook to balance, work on latch hook or crewel, hem pants (I always count my straight pins!) or write letters. I get a lot accomplished, and it sure beats hassling with them to go to bed.
S. Schuessler, Barrington, IL

I tell my 3-year-old that if he doesn't take a nap, which he hates, he has to go to bed at a certain time. It's his decision, and when the time comes, he doesn't fuss too much. I remind him that it was his decision, not mine, for him to go to bed.
Cynthia Wagner, Montebello, CA

After the light is out, we lie on our 3-year-old's bed with him and wait until he goes to sleep, usually in about 10 minutes. My husband nearly always ends up falling asleep, too, and he doesn't mind the early evening nap! Ian looks forward to the "snuggly time," and so do we.
Donna Carswell, Pittsburgh, PA

When I put our 3½-year-old and our 16½-month-old twins to bed, I rub their backs gently and talk softly as they settle down. It seems to ease the transition between active wake time and sleep time. I tell each how special he or she is to us and that we love them. If our older son has helped me during the day, I tell him I appreciate it and thank him. It takes so little time, even for all three, and makes them feel warm, loved and secure—good feelings to go to sleep on.
Joyce Jacobsen, St. Edward, NB

Our biggest problems have always been with overtired kids. When our 8-year-old was a baby, we discovered she slept better and went to bed easier on days when she'd had a nap. The treatment has worked for all five of our children. Our 13-month-old twins take three naps a day; our 3½-year-old still takes a 2-hour nap. All five sleep almost 12 hours a night with no fuss at bedtime.
Catherine Poulos, Park Ridge, IL

Our 4-year-old gave up naps at 2 and still resisted bedtime. Ritual became the key word. ALWAYS: 1) bathroom, 2) brush teeth, 3) share a story, 4) goodnight! Now that she is older, we let her play a radio QUIETLY to lull her to sleep.
Judy Deuel, West Bloomfield, MI

I feel children need "fair warning" and don't like to be pulled away from their activities abruptly, so I use a kitchen timer to let them know how much time is theirs before bedtime. This is my way of respecting their activities and allowing them to respect my word, successful with all my daughters, now 14½, 13, 10½ and 6. (It also works for getting chores done and getting places on time!)
Carol Kenzy, Sunbury, PA

My 7-year-old-son used to like to be sung to sleep. If I had a nickel for every off-key Peter, Paul and Mary ballad I warbled for him, I'd be writing this from Maui. Now that he's older, all he wants is a debate to stall for time.
Mary Schultz, Rochester MI

I don't think of it as a "ritual" or "technique." We live on a second-shift shedule, and it's flexible. We've never had hassles because we keep one rule in mind: you can't make them sleep if they're not tired. I can pretty well tell when they are ready to settle down.
Jeanne Cox, Peoria, IL

I put them to bed—night light on and close the door—and tune them out!
Nancee Teresi, Santa Cruz, CA

THE PERSONS HARDEST TO CONVINCE THAT IT'S TIME TO RETIRE ARE CHILDREN AT BEDTIME.

parents forum

David Lock (Exley Publishing, UK)

Q How have you dealt with monsters and nightmares?

Books mentioned by various parents as being helpful in dealing with children's night fears are: MY MAMA SAYS THERE AREN'T ANY ZOMBIES, GHOSTS, VAMPIRES(etc.), by Judith Viorst (Atheneum, $1.95); THERE'S A NIGHTMARE IN MY CLOSET, by Mercer Mayer (Dial, $6,95); the "Little Monster" books by the same author; and WHERE THE WILD THINGS ARE, by Maurice Sendak (Harper and Row, $5.95). Also mentioned as being helpful were all the Sesame Street materials.

I am reminded of a story of a little girl who repeatedly woke up and came into her parents' room to sleep. After taking her back into her room several times and saying, "Don't be afraid, Jesus is with you," the father finally gave up and said angrily, "If you come in here again, you're getting a spanking." In a few minutes he heard her sobbing in her room and went in and asked, "What's the matter, don't you believe Jesus is with you?" His daughter said, "Yes, but right now I need someone with skin on!"

Pam Matthews, Centerville, TX

We tell him repeatedly that monsters are imaginary, but sometimes he'll say something about a monster and I'll say, "Well, invite him in for cookies," because I'd heard he was a good monster and I wanted to meet him. Treating it in an ordinary way seems to lessen the fear.

Mrs. M. Jung, Austin, TX

When our son went through a period of bad dreams we would wash his face with a warm washcloth to be sure he was wide awake. Then he'd be OK—right back to sleep.

Darla Penney, Superior, WI

My husband always plays monster with the kids, so they don't think of monsters in a negative way. We've never teased them about monsters or the boogy man. With nightmares, I cuddle them until they settle down and fall back asleep—usually in a few minutes.

Bobbie Spallina, Oak Lawn, IL

Our 3-year-old has a fit if his light is turned off. We argued over this for awhile and then I just decided, where is it written that you MUST sleep with the light off? For his comfort and peace of mind, I leave it on.

Susan Lipke, Harrietta, MI

Pull the bed away from the wall so shadows can't touch, and get a window shade that won't let light in.

Bev Spindler, Roseville, MI

We usually say prayers with our son at night and tell him to talk with God if he gets scared. We also leave a light on in the closet, with the door partly open so he can see. He says monsters come out of dark closets, so with the closet lit up he doesn't have to worry.

Dana Clark, Santa Barbara, CA

Our son sleeps in a crib with one side removed and pushed up against our bed. When he wakes from a nightmare, he crawls over to me and I hug him and we both fall asleep. Sometimes a bottle of milk calms him down. We leave a night light on so he won't have to wake in darkness. I also utter a lot of, "Mommie is here; everything is all right; I love you."

Connie Tenn, West Linn, OR

We try to replace bad thoughts with good, and name all the things that make us happy. We learned this from SOUND OF MUSIC.

Carol Taylor, Birmingham, AL

When our daughter has a bad dream I rock her and try to get her to tell me about it. When she is ready to go back to bed, I turn her pillow over, because the bad dream is on that side. She now has a fresh side with no bad dreams on it. This little thing seems to help her get back to sleep easily.

Susan Cooper, Franklin, MA

I never belittle my child for her fears, for obviously to her they are far from trivial. However, I would never give credence to her fear by "sweeping the snakes away" or "shooing the monsters out of the bedroom." I acknowledge the fear and she receives my sympathetic ear. I always emphasize the difference between fears and reality.

Mrs. R. Gould, Milwaukee, WI

We handle "monsters" realistically—we've sprayed them away with aerosol spray cans, blown them out the window, flushed them down the toilet and thrown them out in the garbage. I have a friend who even has her dog come into the room to eat them up.

Mary Ann Lindsey, New York, NY

BOOK AND AUDIO TAPE TO THE RESCUE!

Shows you how to read your baby's unique sleep patterns; how to gently alter your baby's feeding and sleeping schedule to suit your own; how to "set the stage" and help a fussy baby drop off to sleep; the best bedtime routines for older babies and toddlers and much more.

Audio tape offers music and stimulated womb sounds to put your baby to sleep. Parent tested; it works!

SOMETIMES GETTING YOUR BABY TO SLEEP— AND BACK TO SLEEP—SEEMS LIKE THE IMPOSSIBLE DREAM.

parents forum

Bicycle Safety

Q How and where did your child learn to ride a bike?

First by waiting until the desire was really there. My 6½-year-old learned in two evenings last summer. My husband just kept running back and forth following Brandon. Brandon was elated by the time it was over. My husband was exhausted!

Dee Lewin, Southfield, MI

At 4½ she spent a very industrious month with a very small two-wheeler, no training wheels. She's ridden since.

Unsigned

Waiting until *he* was ready, until he asked to learn and asked for help, then letting his brother help him, as I have no patience with running after a bike.

Linda Ferris, Mandeville, LA

My son learned when he was 6½. Training wheels really didn't help, because he would wobble from side to side and didn't feel confident. We took the boy's bar off so he could jump off easier without hurting himself. Also we didn't rush him to learn to ride; if he asked for help we were there, but we didn't force him to learn to ride for us.

Sandy Long, Santa Ana, CA

I have found it helps to put my husband in charge of this job (plus wait until the child is ready and interested). These are his recommendations: 1) Get a small bike (no training wheels, ever). 2) *Be in good shape!* 3) Grasp the bike seat and child's shoulder. 4) Run alongside on level road or slight downgrade. 5) Now, for the hard part—helping the child start and stop. Joe suggests the child wear long pants for falls!

Karen Gromada, Cincinnati, OH

Two boys—two ways of learning. Our 5-year-old learned first. We had him straddle the bike and lift his legs to feel balance and *unbalance*. Then we started him down our slightly inclined drive, and he took it from there.

Our 3-year-old is a real bull. He did it all by himself; and, after a month of watching him ride, it still makes the hair on the back of my neck stand up!

Kathy Kickok, Delray Beach, FL

The way I learned as a child was the basic push-kid-down-street-and-watch-her-crash routine. But I learned in one day. I think the main problem is that *the child forgets to keep pedaling!*

Sandy Heath, Brownsville, TX

On the beach . . . falling can be as much fun as riding!

Sharon Stitt, Seattle, WA

I helped my son learn to ride a two-wheeler by driving my son and my husband to a large vacant parking lot and returning one hour later. It took my 7-year-old about a week to master this skill.

Nedra O'Neill, Calumet Park, IL

No special techniques—just a fast running husband ready to grab the bike if needed.

Susan Antell, Kansas City, MO

We waited until they were physically and emotionally ready. Peer pressure also gives them the enthusiasm to learn. I personally don't push this particular activity. (I worry so much.) I managed to keep my son off the street 'til he was 7—when his friends teased him about it.

Jerri Oyama, Northridge, CA

• Impress upon your child that a bike is a vehicle—like a car—and not a toy. The rules of the road must be obeyed. Stress the fact that ignorance of the rules and carelessness can cause accidents, even death.
• Attach a tall flag (bright orange is easiest to see) to the bike to warn drivers and pedestrians that THERE'S A CHILD HERE.
• Put reflector tape on prominent spots of the bike if the child will ever ride at dusk or at night. Add some tape to a jacket, too. And remember that light-colored clothing is easiest for drivers to see.
• Have the child wear clips to keep clothing from getting caught in bike gears. You can make inexpensive ones by attaching Velcro to heavy ribbon or tape.
• Buy a good basket so the child won't be tempted to steer with one hand while holding something in the other.
• Supply a helmet. Bicycle accidents are the leading cause of serious head and neck injuries in children, and bicycle helmets do save lives.

from *Vicki Lansky's Practical Parenting Tips for Parents of School-Age Kids*

My 7-year-old boy was scared of it and not doing too well until a smaller friend got up on my son's bike and rode it all over. After that, my son practiced like mad and in one day was able to ride—and loves it!

Leigh Galey, Metairie, LA

I will be starting this project this spring. I've learned one thing from my neighbors: parents get more exercise than their children do. I realized this as I watched them running beside or behind their child's wobbly bike!

Debbie Ulrich, Lewiston, MN

Gay Courter-Reprinted with permission.

parents forum

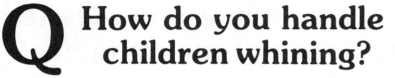

Q How do you handle children whining?

I ask him what he needs. I look at whining as a need to express pent-up emotions. I encourage him to cry if that's what he needs or to beat up a pillow or talk—or see if he's hungry, tired, etc.
Michele McBrayer   Georgetown, KY

I try to prevent it. For example, my 5-year-old gets whiny when he comes home hungry from preschool and I'm too busy with the baby to fix his lunch right away. So I've started fixing his lunch box so it will be ready for him when he gets home.
Natalie Warren   Columbus, OH

I stop what I'm doing and listen carefully to see if I can do anything about the problem. If I can't, I change the subject or find something that will interest and distract her. If nothing works, I remind myself that I have days like that, too.
Judy LeMay   S. Burlington, VT

I put my hands over my ears and say, "Ooh, that tone hurts Mommy's ears. I can only listen to *smiling* voices!"
Kathy S.   Burbank, IL

I tell my daughter (2½) that I can't hear her when she whines and that if she wants something she will have to use her nice voice. When she was younger I sent her to her room until she was through. Now that she is older, we talk about emotions a lot. I say, "You sound mad because your toy is stuck," or "You sound sad because I won't give you a cookie." Now she will come to me and say, "I'm sad," or "I'm angry" and that will get us started talking about her problem.
Ann Schuster   St. Paul, MN

I ignore it. When my son stops whining, I reward him. He's learning that whining gets no results, whereas nice behavior does.
Rita McTamney   Baltimore, MD

When my daughter spoke to me, she would go from talking, to teasing, to nagging and whining—and I would get angry. Finally, I realized that I wasn't *looking* at her until I was angry at her. Now I make sure we have eye contact any time she's talking to me, and she doesn't get frustrated enough to whine as often. We are polite enough to look at adults who speak to us, why not children?
Unsigned

I use "I" messages: "I get a headache when you whine." If my son really understands how his behavior affects me, he tends to adjust what he does.
Jeri Wilkes   Puyallup, WA

I sing "Happy Talk" from *South Pacific* or ask if she can please ask in a nicer way. She gets the idea eventually.
Susan Keck   Gaithersburg, MD

I hate whining! My sister was a whiner and I swore that no child of mine would be one. But my daughter (7) is. When she starts to whine, I say, "I can't understand you when you talk like that. Take a deep breath and start over." It usually works. Even her brother and sister tell her!
MaryEllen Cooper   Glendale, AZ

I used to get impatient with whining, but then I realized that it only happened when I wasn't paying enough attention to them. So now their whining reminds me that it's time to unplug the iron and get out a storybook. The break does us all good!
Gina Walker   Hickory Hills, IL

I have always hated whining. Now that my son is 12, we imitate "The Whiners" from *Saturday Night Live* when we are feeling cranky, and we end up laughing at ourselves.
Jane Beckwith   Pittsburg, PA

When my child whines, I feed him; 90 percent of the time it seems he was just hungry.
Jill Heasley   Fresno, CA

First I decide if I want them to do or have whatever they're whining for. If yes, then I tell them to ask in a nice, cheerful voice. Otherwise, I tell them no and that even if they ask me a thousand times, the answer will still be no. I *never* give in. It works.
Judy Cherin   Chicago, IL

When telling him to stop and ignoring him don't work, I send him to his room for a time-out. This seems to work well.
Jeanne Conley   Sherrill, IA

The 11th Commandment: Whine Not

Q: Who is often seen with clenched fists, bugged-out eyes, and hair on end?
A: The parent of a whiner.

When asked when his child started talking, one parent replied: "Oh, he didn't talk until he was five. Before that, all he did was whine."

Also called the water-dripping-on-a-stone trick, whining is employed by kids for the purpose of getting something or somewhere. If it works, then it was worth the effort, and will be tried again. With a lot of persistence, parents can demonstrate this habit will not work any more.

How to respond to a whiner

• First look for physical causes. Perhaps the child is tired or needs a pick-me-up snack.

• If you feel the urge to give in, do so immediately. Then the kid will not learn that longevity of the attack guarantees success.

• Show that while whining will not work, a pleasant voice will. "That voice you're using really bothers my ears. Could you use your regular voice?"

• When, all on their own, children ask for something in a pleasant way, and if it is a request you can honor, respond quickly and amiably: "I'd be happy to. How nice you were to ask in such a pleasant voice."

• Make sure you have been listening to the child. Children often whine or nag because they have to: it's the only way to get the adult's attention.

• To the persistent request for the denied toy or snack, reply, "My answer is final. I am not going to talk any more about it." Then by all means, don't talk about it.

• Make sure *your* requests are congenial. Often we reinforce whining by the examples we set.

Diane Mason

parents forum paren

Q How and at what ages have you weaned your children? Any special techniques?

Whether weaning from breast or bottle, pacifier, whatever . . . your experiences confirm once again that there is NO ONE WAY to handle your children. You do what's right for YOU, and even then you can't guarantee that you wouldn't do it differently, given the chance. For some, gradual, loving separation works. For others, letting the child take the lead is right. And for still others, action by the parent is what makes sense.

My son was small and active and constantly hungry. At a year he still woke regularly for a night feeding. Daddy and I had a system: I got baby and settled into the rocker. He fixed the bottle and brought it to us. The baby was finally sleeping through occasionally and we were actually enjoying a good night's sleep again. One night he called again. I settled into the rocker with him; Dad brought the bottle and poured it in our laps—he had forgotten to put the top on! That did it. The baby has slept through the night ever since.

Shirley Riley, Seattle, WA

I weaned my baby at six months by gradually substituting a bottle. My great savior was giving her a bottle AND me from the very start. She bottle-fed with a sitter and was breastfed with me, so weaning was no big deal. The bottle wasn't strange to her. I find babies very adjustable and the combination worked grand for both of us.

Karen Leitch, Calgary, Alta.

Sarah weaned herself by 12½ months, much to my surprise and distress. My basic advice is to be prepared to feel unwanted and unloved and to rejoice in another step forward.

Mrs. Leslie Bricker, Ann Arbor, MI

THERE'S A SUCKER BORN EVERY MINUTE! P. T. Barnum

When my first was ready to give up her bottle I kept giving it to her, out of habit. Pay attention to the kid! Children will let you know when they're ready to quit.

Pam Huntsman, Emerson, IA

Wean when the child is ready: child-led weaning. I know, I know . . . not what you had in mind. Children are people and deserve being treated as such.

Shirley Sparks, Shelby, NB

A hint to help cut down on toddler nursing: tell a child over 18 months that he or she may nurse until you count to 20, and then stop. If you are in a hurry, you can reach 20 very quickly. Otherwise, count slowly.

Karen Gromada, Cincinnati, OH

My son was weaned from nursing at 14 months. (Sage tea helped stop the flow of milk and going back on birth control pills helps, too.) But now, at 3 years, I can't wean him from his night bottle!

Unsigned, from Portland, OR

My first three were weaned at 5 months, 3 months and 3 months, and I am so enlightenedly sad I did it—their baby seasons were SO SHORT, and allergies abounded. Now, 17 years later, my fourth (3) and I are still a very happy nursing couple. When he gets banged up, instead of nursing the hurt away, he wants to put his "picnics" on the sore place. Is that a testamonial or what!

Merrie Ann Handley, Boulder Creek, CA

I had to stop nursing my second daughter at 7 months because of her BITING—she even drew blood. NOTHING would get her to stop. I had no trouble switching her from bottle to cup; she just seemed to enjoy using a cup.

Barbara Sattora, Rush, NY

Weaned from the breast at 10 months—we both got bored! From the bottle at 13 months. She had diarrhea, so one night I put 7-Up in her bottle, the next night I skipped the bottle, and that was it.

Anita Whisney, Alpha, MN

My 15-month old doesn't nurse any more, BUT he needs to have my breast exposed to hang onto. He pulls my blouse up when we sit down for a bottle. I intend to let nature take its course and hope he quits before he's 20.

Maureen Morriston, Ft. Mitchell, KY

My only suggestion is to wait until the baby is ready. When my baby got less interested in nursing, at about 16 months, I started walking with her and pushing her around the house in her stroller, doing things that she liked but that didn't involve nursing. I also lay on the bed with her and rocked her, but in positions that least emphasized nursing.

Karen Haynes, Albuquerque, NM

David Lock (Exley Publishing, UK)

Invest in a heating pad! I weaned our son at 13 months by gradually dropping a feeding a week. Had terrible problems with clogged ducts (very painful) for which the usual solution is to nurse more often. I had no problems after I started using the heating pad. I dragged my heels about starting weaning because of the "emotional attachment," but discovered that once I got through it I really didn't miss nursing as much as I thought I would. My son doesn't miss it at all!

Debbie Schoepper, Troutdale, OR

Neither of my daughters ever demonstrated any signs of self-weaning, so I led the way both times, slowly and with love, starting when they were about 1½. I picked the least necessary (to me) nursing and offered drinks and snacks and spent extra time cuddling and playing. Then I picked the next least desirable, and so on. I was in no rush, so spaced each elimination at least two weeks apart. I was never uncomfortable and the girls adapted well. I am sad to finish nursing my youngest, but look forward to the freedom of having her dad put her to bed at night.

Unsigned

One summer day I told my daughter (3½) that if she was old enough to chew gum she was too old to nurse. She said, "OK, I want gum," and never asked to nurse again. So she threw me over for a package of sugar-free bubblegum—talk about rejection!

Rosemarie Schmid, Pennsville, NJ

forum parents forum

My daughter weaned herself from the bottle at just about a year. At first I was terribly worried that she wasn't getting enough milk—she went from three or four 8-ounce bottles a day to just a couple of ounces from a cup at meals. My doctor told me to relax, as long as the rest of her diet was well-balanced. She was right; in about a month, my daughter was drinking lots more from the cup and she's never been healthier.

Janet Cooper, Pittsburgh, PA

For weaning a child from the bottle, try switching to straws (colored ones are fun). I've seen cups shaped like animals with straw holes—less chance for spills.

Joan Pace, Fairfax, CA

I don't understand why anyone would want to wean to a bottle or pacifier, since the baby would have to be weaned from them, too. I weaned our children gradually, dropping one feeding at a time.

Debbie Gunderson, Scottville, MI

We finally tried a Nuk nipple, and it worked. At first we had to have her dad feed her with it and pretend I wasn't home!

Marge Korsi, Milwaukee, WI

Teaching a child to use a cup was murder until I found the Tupperware lids with little holes (Sippy Seals). They work great and are just like drinking from a regular cup except that the seal regulates the flow and prevents spills. They're even good when Daddy is sick in bed.

Beth Schapira, Mesa, AZ

Our boy had turned 2 and was still clinging to his bottle at bedtime. Finally we talked with him about what was to happen the next day: we were going to gather all the bottles and throw them in the trash because "Ryan is a big boy and doesn't need them anymore." To our surprise, he helped put them all in the bag and threw it in the wastebasket himself. It's important for the child to at least see it being done so he knows they're really gone. (They can be retrieved later, when the child's not around, and hidden for use with another child).

Kris Chadek, APO NY

Ed. note: That reminds us of a "bottle-tossing party," complete with a special meal and a new cup wrapped for the child to open, which we read about in THE MOTHER TO MOTHER BABY CARE BOOK, by Barbara Sills and Jeanne Henry (Avon, $5.95).

When Your Children Were Weaned

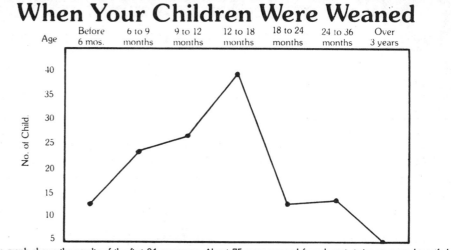

The graph shows the results of the first 34 responses. About 75 were weaned from breast; twice as many breastfed children went directly to cup as to bottle.

Confessions of a Late-Nursing Mom

David will be three in a week. "Nummy" is his all-purpose word for my breasts, breast milk and breastfeeding. Despite what he claims, I know that the "nummies" are almost dry, although the sweet trickle that remains is enough to remind him of his babyhood, comfort him when he's anxious and lure him back for more—usually about once a day. Some days he forgets.

While I now accept the fact that my preschool aged son still nurses, I did not always have such a liberal attitude about weaning. I instinctively *knew* I would breastfeed my babies, but I never imagined I would nurse a walking, talking child. During my first pregnancy, in fact, I was horrified by a three-foot-high suckling boy who nursed repeatedly while his mother led my introductory La Leche League meeting. The scene assaulted my pastel daydreams of nourishing my expected infant in rocking chair seclusion.

These preconceptions faded during the twenty-one months I nursed David's older sister, Michelle. After I overcame engorgement, tender nipples and the fear that I would smother her, breastfeeding was incredibly lovely. . . .

David arrived when Michelle was 4, and I happily embarked on the same nursing course, aware that he could continue for several years but assuming he would follow Michelle's precedent. He did not. The longer he nursed, the more concerned I became about when he would stop. My faith in child-led weaning's benefits remains intact, but mothering a late weaner has not been easy. With the special rewards of nursing my son for such an extended period have come criticism, conflicts between my needs and

David's and doubts about my motivation for continuing to breastfeed. . . .

I resented David at times, and I felt guilty about it. I had taken a two-year leave of absence from teaching to care for him, but after sixteen months I grew impatient to return to work. . . . I made every effort to be resourceful when he was upset—trying to distract him, rock him or offer him a drink—but nursing remained the most effective pacifier. In some instances I was grateful that I *could* console him; at other times I longed for an alternative. . . . Perhaps I was artificially extending David's dependency because he completed our two-child family. . . .

Author's Postscript: David weaned himself soon after his third birthday. Ironically, when I realized he hadn't nursed for several days, I could not remember the final time. After about a week, a teasing tone in his voice, he asked for "nummy" again. With surprising ease, I told him honestly that he no longer needed to nurse, and he accepted my response. He repeated his request a few times in the days that followed; my answer remained consistent and he never pressed me. Then it was over. . . .

Now, four months since David has stopped nursing, my breasts look small and flaccid. Last night in the shower I checked to see whether any milk remained. Several creamy drops splashed down my body, mixing with warm water and sudden tears.

From THE MOTHERS' BOOK: SHARED EXPERIENCES, edited by Ronnie Friedland and Carol Kort, published by Houghton Mifflin Company, Boston. Copyright © 1981 by Ronnie Friedland and Carol Kort. Reprinted by permission of Houghton Mifflin Company. The book may be ordered by mail for $10.95 ppd from the publisher, 2 Park Street, Boston, MA 02108.

parents forum

Q What works for you when bathing and shampooing scared children?

This question is one more parents than not seem to have dealt with, though it's not much spoken about. The most common solution given was to simply get into the bath with the child. While this works for many, the range of ideas gives other alternatives.

For shampooing, I tried songs, smiles, silly noises. None of them worked, but a string of bells with different tones really does the trick. I hang them above her (she's 3½ months) where I can reach them with one hand and hold her with the other.
> *Darla Finney*
> *Coeur d' Alene, ID*

A wet washcloth on my daughter's tummy calms her when she's being laid back for a shampoo. She sucks water from it, and it takes her mind off her fears.
> *Diana Crawford*
> *Portage, MI*

To wash my 3½-year-old son's hair, we use only about an inch and a half of water in the tub so he can lie down flat on the bottom. Putting cotton in his ears helps, too.
> *Sue Taylor*
> *Memphis, TN*

Swimming goggles or face masks keep soap and water out of eyes and distract kids until the bath and shampoo are over.
> *Beverley Spindler*
> *Roseville, MI*

Using a sponge instead of a cup to rinse hair makes you able to control the water better, avoiding eyes and ears.
> *Suzanne Magsig*
> *Royal Oak, MI*

I shampooed my son in the tub, with a detachable shower head. I folded a small towel for him to hold over his face, and to distract him, we'd sing his favorite songs and make up new ones. Cacophonous, but effective!
> *Mary Schultz*
> *Rochester, MI*

I even resorted to taking a bath without 15-month-old daughter. It didn't help. Time did, though!
> *Mrs. J. Rupprecht*
> *Sanborn, MN*

As a swimming instructor, I find teaching swimming techniques the perfect opportunity at bath time. The first thing a child notices is water temperature – very important at an early age. Then, if they learn the "trick" of splashing for Mom, they are not afraid of splashes at the pool. The Red Cross book TEACHING JOHNNY TO SWIM is good. And a tight, firm grip gives a child a secure feeling.
> *Penny Miller*
> *Marshalltown, IA*

With my oldest, I used a bath seat with suction cups on the bottom and a strap. That seemed to reassure her until she was about 2½ – and afraid of the dreaded hair wash. I have found that water (a lot, anyway) on the face seems to be one of the biggest offenders, as well as the sound of running water. Best to fill the tub before bringing the child in. Others are afraid of the draining, though I found my own relieved to see the water go!
> *Deborah Smollen*
> *Middlefield, CT*

David Lock (Exley Publishing, UK)

Let an older child sit in the tub in an outgrown infant seat. It tilts on an angle, and the child's head can be tipped back comfortably.
> *Peg Stickney*
> *Plymouth, MI*

Use a non-skid mat, lots of floating toys and bubble bath (but only occasionally – some children break out from it and it can contribute to vaginal infections in girls).
> *Lee Moran*
> *Cortland, OH*

I put my 6- and 3-year-olds on the ironing board, and their heads hang over the wash tubs in the basement. I hold their heads and wash away with a shampoo sprayer.
> *Jean Marie Urban Garfield Hts., OH*

My son was *very* afraid, so we decreased his baths to two a week. My husband and I bathed with him, and recently (at 22 months) he asked for a bath—SUCCESS! We've learned to keep cool and not force—he's coming out of a lot of fears now because we've not placed our worries on his shoulders.
> *Dawn Lee Bettendorf, IA*

There are two hard times in a child's life when bathing and shampooing are particularly fearsome—ages 9 to 11 months and 2½ to 3 years. I shampoo as little as possible during these periods, brushing hair often and washing it with a damp washcloth. When absolutely necessary, I bathe and shampoo them as quickly and matter-of-factly as possible, praising them for their "bravery" in the face of soap and water. Making soap sculptures in shampooed hair before a mirror is sometimes effective. They do get over fear, and soon it's back to wiping up the bathroom floor after "swimming parties."
> *Pam Pierre Minnetonka, MN*

Hair Care

- Sit your child in a high chair to prevent "wandering." Spread a newspaper underneath.
- Remove gum from hair with peanut butter. Work it into the hair and then comb out the gum and peanut butter.

parentsforum

Q What advice do you have for eartube preparation?

We had tubes inserted in the oldest at 3½ years. His speach had been very slow. We saw a dramatic improvement. The youngest got tubes at 14 months. His otitis wouldn't resond to antibiotics. Now at 20-months, his speech is unbelievable, and we've had no further problems with otitis. Both children toured the hospital, saw a movie and were given a bag of goodies. When the actual surgery occurred, they were given a box of crayons, books, stickers, etc., which kept them busy and calm. We also played hospital the previous week many times using and old Fisher-Price play-children's hospital.
Susan Wells   Rockwood, TN

My son, Daniel was two weeks shy of his first birthday when he had tubes inserted. He had had nine ear infections in as many months and one was unresolved for two months. His surgery was very nicely handled. They had a nurse come and play with him for a few minutes before taking him to be anesthesized. He went willingly and laughlingly. I was the first person he saw when he woke up in recovery and we were home a few hours later.
Denise Voeller   Coon Rapids, MN

After five ear infections in two years, I asked my pediatrician if he recommended ear tubes for my 4-year-old. He said some parents decide in favor of surgery to avoid keeping their child on antibiotics during repeated infections. His advice was to wait until age five when my son would probably outgrow the condition. He did and I'm glad we waited. I would rather have my child take antibiotics temporarily than face unnecessary surgery.
Janet Stabile   Ellington, CN

Although our daughter had several ear infections we avoided tubes with the help of our pediatrician who agreed with us that ear tubes were not the answer. Most children with ear tubes have smoking parents or are in day care, or both.
Alice Horne   Norcross, GA

Our son had tubes at age 20 months. The experience was easier on him than me, of course. He enjoyed all the fun and toys the pediatric ward had to offer. At age 3, he has had no more ear infections and suffering.
Lori Stefanishion   Alberta

He had them around 12 to 14 months. He was too young to know what was going on. Me? I could have used a sedative. It was very traumatic to hand my baby over to the doctors and leave him. The only reassuring thought was that I knew he was in good hands.
Pam Stuart   Tulsa, OK

Because of *excessive* infections of the ears and tonsils and apnea, my son had a myringotomy and tonsiladenoidectomy simultaneously at age 4½. The experience was a good one except for the fact he was released after four hours. It was much too soon. More emphasis should have been put on the warning that bleeding may occur after one week. This happened in our case and it was absolutely terrifying! I would do it again though, because he hasn't had a single infection in almost three years.
Kirs Taranec   Lake Havasu, AZ

Both my daughters had eartubes and tonsillectomies at age 4. I know the procedure is controversial, but it turned the health of both daughters around. They are no longer plagued by colds, running noses, etc. We visited the hospital before surgery so that they knew what to expect. To make their lives a bit easier after the surgery, we had custom-made earplugs made by the audiologist in the office of the ENT. We no longer had to worry about baths, showers and swimming. They are simple to insert, safe and very practical.
Nedra O'Neill   Evergreen Park, IL

My son had tubes implanted at 11-months. Prior to the tubes he had ear infections nearly every month. He went from one antibiotic to another, as each one lost its effect. He often had temperatures of 105°. Because of his age there was no way to prepare him for surgery. He really didn't know what was happening, and he was already used to all the ear check ups. The day after his surgery he pulled himself to standing for the first time and was walking only a few weeks later. He started noticing sounds he never had before. I think the constant ear infections affected his balance and hearing.
Kathy Brockman   Sidney, OH

Children and Ear Tube Surgery

Young children are more susceptible to middle ear infections because they are more susceptible to infections in general; upper respiratory infections, in particular. The bacteria or virus that causes these illnesses, in the form of a cold or flu, often lead to infection and inflammation of the middle ear because of the short connection of the Eustachian tubes which join the throat to the middle ear.

When fluid in the middle ear does not subside, despite medical treatment, hearing loss can occur. Hearing loss for any length of time with young children can impede learning, and especially speech development.

Doctors today are recommending ear tubes—the placement tiny PE (pressure-equalization) or tympanostomy tubes—to ventilate and drain the middle ear. These tubes equalize pressure on either side of the ear so fluid cannot readily collect. For many children it also reduces the number of future ear infections.

This procedure involves a very small incision of the ear drum (myringotomy) to drain the ear and place this small hollow ear tube about the size of this dot—o—in the ear drum. It is usually carried out under general anesthesia. It is a simple and short operation that is performed at day-surgery and hospital centers, eliminating the need for an overnight stay.

Because this common surgical procedure requires anesthesia, there are accompanying concerns for both parent and child alike. Knowing what to expect can help you prepare your child and reduce anxiety for both of you. With that in mind, I have written a new KoKo book, *KoKo Bear's Big Ear-Ache* (Bantam) which will be in the bookstores fall of 1987. I'll have more information on this title later in the year.

VL

parents forum

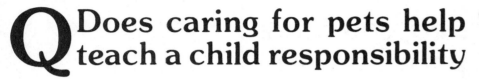

The Virtues of Hermit Crabs

Q Does caring for pets help teach a child responsibility

Pets have been a prime motivating force in teaching my three children responsibility. My oldest son, Aaron, took care of his pet gerbil, Sahara, since he first got her when he was in nursery school. I always had encouraged him to keep a written record of his pets' lives—when they were born, illnesses, size of litters, and record of deaths. His record-keeping paid off when Sahara gained fame as the oldest living caged gerbil in the *Guiness Book of World Records*. Pets teach children the whole cycle of life and death.

Currently, Aaron, who is now fourteen, is planning a scientific experiment breeding gerbils of different colors. My middle son is raising Japanese quail.

We also have a cat and a colony of giant South American cockroaches which we raise and donate to various schools in our area.

My nine-year-old daughter is the class authority on slugs, as the one she captured in our garden in late summer is still alive and has since given birth to a family of baby slugs. We've always felt there is room in everyone's life for a pet, since our children have learned so much from taking care of their animals. Children who have allergies to fur can always raise fish, insects, or reptiles. *Great Pets* by Sara Stein (Workman Publishing Co., $5.95) is an excellent large-size paperback book on all kinds of pets and their care.

Sidney Milstone, Lathrup Village, MI

We live on a farm, and Mary (3½) has learned by example. Thank goodness our cats and dog like to be hugged. She also chases chickens and has a special friend—the only black chicken we have, who she hugs. (Ugh!)

Lisa Schickedanz, Gage, OK

I do volunteer work rehabilitating orphaned and injured birds. Watching the constant essential care they must have, and hearing the reasons why they must not become pets but remain wild, has been more effective in teaching responsibility and a true understanding of animals than I think any pet ever could.

Jeannette Ralston, Sunnyvale, CA

Oh, sure. He took it so seriously that he promptly fed his goldfishes three meals a day. (Of course, they died from overeating!) Now, if I can find a pet that doesn't mind eating three meals a day . . . .

Unsigned

My daughter is too young to fully understand responsibility, but having a dog since she was born has been very beneficial, I believe, because she has learned to be gentle with animals and *she* isn't *always* the center of attention. She follows our example of being loving toward an animal. She also has no fear of any other friends.

Cindy Weber, Milwaukee, WI

One of the tenets of parenthood is that children need pets. Some parents, who do not wish to deny their kids the pleasures and responsibilities of owning a pet, seek a simpler solution.

Enter the hermit crab. This fascinating little crustacean has a soft abdomen, and, in order to protect it, lives in an abandoned shell. He's cheap to buy and feed, is easy to care for, and fun to watch. He is also a unique show-and-tell items easily transported to school and stuck in a corner to be admired at leisure during the day.

Hermit crabs vary in size and cost, but usually are inexpensive enough for children to buy themselves. Most pet stores sell small, medium, and large crabs, with prices ranging from about $3.50 to $7 each.

Home for the hermit crab is a bowl or small aquarium with high slippery sides: He's a real escape artist. Decor is simple; a little water, some gravel, a few rocks or a branch, and an extra shell or two. Extra shells should be larger than the one the crab is living in. If he grows bigger and molts, he'll need to switch shells.

One drawback as a pet: It doesn't show a lot of affection. On the other hand, it also doesn't bark, chase cars, get stuck in trees, or make its owner presents of dead mice. There's something to be said for that.

Extracts from an article by Breck Longstreth in Seattle's Child, June, 1983

Having had a dog from the time he was born, our 3-year-old has never been afraid of dogs, and absolute loves them. In the past few weeks, he has developed a fear of cats, though. I'm not sure why, but I have read that "animal fears" often crop up at age 3. He is very stoic about it, and I can tell when he sees someone on the block with a pet cat that he is forcing himself to go up and see it but is very tentative about the whole process. (He used to play with them as freely as he does dogs.) Any insights into "sudden" fears?

Sandy Heath, Brownsville, TX

We had a beagle puppy for our 4-year-old son and 1-year-old daughter. Disaster! The dog howled for fourteen nights in spite of all efforts, chewed up everything, and growled and snapped at our daughter because she petted him in his bed when he wanted to be alone. Got rid of the dog. *Never* again!

Leigh Galey, Metairie, LA

"I've never had pet fish before. How do you make the newspaper stay on the bottom of the tank?"

Reprinted by permission of V. Gene Myers

It's nice for children to have pets—until the pets start having children!

parentsforum

Q How have you helped your child overcome shyness?

We started an informal play group of five children, aged 2 to 2½, who meet once a week for two hours. The regularity of our little "school" has helped the children learn to play with others and to deal with different adults and has eased fears of being separated from Mother.

Judi Welsh, Apply Valley, MN

I try to build self-esteem. I feel that a positive self concept is the best basis for social competence.

N. Warren, Columbus, OH

My 20-month-old triplets have the opposite problem—they're the biggest hams you ever saw! I think they feel secure with one another and they're usually fine even when separated.

Kathie Sedwick, Oceano, CA

I've accepted my 6-year-old's shyness for years and have not pushed to overcome it, but I do discuss with him what he might do in a certain situation. Now he will often strike up a conversation with a stranger (in my presence).

W. Strack, Cleveland, OH

The few times my 4-year-old has been shy have been when strangers or unfamiliar adults have asked his name or age or what's the latest he's been doing or saying. I think he feels that it's his business. Everyone deserves his own private space.

Denise Shea, Vicksburg, MS

My problem is in the other direction—how to teach my child NOT to tell others to stop smoking, eating junk food and such things.

Shirley Cohn, Burnaby, BC

My boy wasn't camera shy—he just hates flashes. When we switched to ASA 400 film indoors, without the flash attachment, all was well.

Connie Tenn, West Linn, OR

Sometimes children think they have to perform or be clever around adults. I just tell my son to smile, shake hands and answer when being spoken to.

Cynthia Wagner, Montebello, CA

Nine out of ten times "scare" is the real feeling behind shyness. Once that is out in the open, we talk about scary feelings and find no real basis for them. Lots of reassurance and very little pushing also help.

Nedra O'Neill, Calumet Park, IL

I insist that people don't force themselves on my daughter (2) and I let her cling to me until she feels secure enough to venture out.

Lisa Smith, Hurst, TX

I have often read that picking your child up so he or she can be at an adult's eye level can ease introductions. When my daughter is being introduced to another child, I stoop down to their level.

Gail Goldberg, Northridge, CA

I think shyness is something you have to accept as part of your child's personality. When my 3½-year-old was an infant, he loved to watch other babies but didn't reach out to them. As a toddler, he was frightened of his more active playmates who careened into him in play. In nursery school, he observes groups of children but usually doesn't join them. He assesses each social situation and decides for himself whether or not it's safe for him to participate in. No amount of prodding will change his mind if he decides it's not safe. I try to arrange as many "safe" activities as I can for him, mostly get-togethers with just one other child. I don't think shyness hurts a child as much as it bothers his parents.

Pat Brinkmann, Palo Alto, CA

Shyness Means Low Self-Esteem

Shyness tends to go hand-in-hand with low self-esteem. Although shy people may value some skill or special ability they may possess, most are their own worst critics. Paradoxically, one source of this poor self-image comes from the high standards shy people tend to set for themselves. They are always coming up short when the yardstick is measured in units of perfection.

Ideally, the relationship between parent and child should enable the child to develop a sense of identity that is anchored in a firm belief in his or her own self-worth. Where love is not given freely, then love is given conditionally for doing the "right thing." Under such conditions, ego and self-respect are put on the line every time the child, and later the adult, takes some action. The message is clear: You are only as good as your most recent success, but never better than the sum of all your failures. Approval, acceptance, and love are thus seen as commodities exchangeable for "desirable behavior." And most frightening, they can be taken away at a moment's notice for doing the wrong thing.

From THE SHY CHILD, by Philip Zimbardo and Shirley Radl (McGraw-Hill, $11.95).

DON'T PUSH! Many children are not really shy, just cautious. If not pushed, they will usually relax, after surveying the situation, and make contact at their own speed. If pushed, they only retreat further.

Sarah Hoback, Albers, IL

We've had best results by telling our 3-year-old that everyone is shy sometimes and that it's OK to be shy. That seems to free her from pressures. Then we suggest things she could do, like show off a doll, and the focus is shifted from HER to the OBJECT.

Kathy Darnell, Hueytown, AL

I've had the opposite problem with my daughter, 3. She's outgoing and sociable, and it's not been unusual for her to strike up a friendship with another child in a store and do everything but get in the car and go home with that child. Many times I've lost her this way in a department store. Any suggestions?

Mrs. R.E. Neslund, Kingston, NY

We tell our children not to talk to strangers—yet when a stranger says hello to them in our presence, we encourage them to respond. I caught myself doing this and now I don't ask them to say hello, but say it myself.

Linda Trust, Riverside, CA

REMEMBER THAT ONE DAY YOUR CHILDREN WILL FOLLOW YOUR EXAMPLE, NOT YOUR ADVICE

parents forum

Q What are your house rules for acute sibling rivalry?

The only sure cure I've heard of for sibling rivalry is to have only ONE child. My kids are now 8 and 11 and—sorry to say—it's not getting any better, folks! —V.L.

The rules are as follows: Extreme fighting over a toy, the toy gets put up. If it's between themselves, it's time out—they sit for 5 to 30 minutes, depending on the frequency of the behavior.

Nancee Teresi, Santa Cruz, CA

When there are squabbles over toys, I give them a timer and tell them to set it for 5 minutes. When the bell goes off, they become responsible for trading and sharing. Praise children for THEIR OWN accomplishments and try to find special traits of each. Discourage competition between them.

Linda Trust, Riverside, CA

SEPARATION! Separate chairs or separate rooms.

Sandy Klingler, Lebanon, PA

It's not always easy to understand the reason for disagreements, especially since they seem so senseless to an adult. I TRY to show them equal attention, but you know how that goes! No matter how much, someone always feels left out. When a violent fight breaks out, involving hitting and name calling, they are confined to their rooms and forbidden to play with each other 'til they calm down.

Jerri Oyama, Northridge, CA

I do not attach as much importance to the cause of the dispute as I do to the resulting display of behavior. This usually takes the form of a fight or quarrel. Such behavior is not acceptable and the children are separated by either being sent to their rooms or being grounded to different chairs. They are then required to think of another method of approaching the problem. This inevitably leads to communication between the children. Once a dialogue has been established (carefully directed by me) a constructive discussion can take place and the cause for the rivalry can be exposed as being unnecessary.

Mrs. A. Gould, Milwaukee, WI

I have a friend who sends both her kids into the bathroom to settle their differences. They're not allowed out until they're friends again.

Jill Heasley, Fresno, CA

Let them work it out as much as possible without interfering. Fights increase if they know Mom is drawn in. When it gets too hot, I isolate them in different rooms. I find Ginott's BETWEEN PARENT AND CHILD techniques helpful. I'm more a liaison or arbitrator to settle differences than the resented LAW!

Karen Gromada, Cincinnati, OH

Basic premise: Fair is not always equal. If one thinks the other got the better deal, too bad. They don't have to like the situation, but they do have to live with it—they'll be the "lucky one" some other time.

Bev Spindler, Roseville, MI

Our main rule is equal punishment. Those times when we are sure what happened and both deny any wrong doing, they both get it. We spank at times, but prefer not to. We use time out, quiet time on a chair, taking away of privileges and reduction in allowance if they helped enough to earn any. They play together very well some days—other days are another story. We try our best to give them equal affection, but children are such manipulators!

David Cox, Peoria, IL

Sibs go to respective rooms to be alone. The problem arises in a few years when new brother bumps older sister from her room to share with little sister. Where do they go to be alone—the bathroom? The water bill will be outrageous!

Debbie Megginson, Auburn, IL

I can't say, at this point, but from the way things are going with my 3½-year-old and 8-month-old, maybe the rule should be that the younger child is allowed to do whatever he or she wants to the older one, just to get even for the times defense against the older was not possible!

SallyAnn Winterle, St. Paul, MN

I number my two children, "even" and "odd," and they take turns doing things on the odd and even numbered days of the month—sitting by the window, choosing toys first, picking TV shows, even doing chores. With more than two kids, it would be more complicated.

Rita Bikel, Stamford, CT

GREAT NEW TIPS

So many great new tips poured in after the publication of BEST PRACTICAL PARENTING TIPS in 1980 that we just had to share them in a revised and expanded edition of the book. Dressed up in a new cover and 10 pages longer, it's available in bookstores and by mail through PPN (see order form).

Here's a sampling:

• Have a new baby? Let modern technology help you avoid answering the phone when you don't want to. Record the details of the baby's birth on a telephone answering machine and add a message about when is the best time to call.

• Make your own inexpensive baby wipes by thoroughly soaking a roll of strong toilet tissue (not the extra soft kind) in a shallow bowl of baby oil. Pull out the center core and start the roll from the inside. Store in a plastic bag or covered container.

• Remember to serve only finger foods that can be eaten with one hand when you have a party with other parents and their new babies—everyone will have a baby on one arm.

• If you forget your list of sizes when shopping with the children, check for fit in socks by having a child make a fist and wrapping the sock around the fist at the knuckles. If the heel and toe meet, the sock will fit.

• Let a child about to graduate to a big bed use a pillow in the crib for a short time before the move. It will help him or her learn to "center" the body while asleep.

• Help a child stop sucking his or her thumb by putting a kiss in each palm and telling him or her to keep hands CLOSED TIGHT all night to keep the kisses in.

parentsforum

Q When was your child ready to be left alone?

They started playing outside alone when they could tell me boundaries and rules. (I still check on them every 5 to 10 minutes.) My oldest son started staying home alone for 15 to 20 minutes when he was 6. He could tell me what he would do in an emergency. I have found playing, "What would you do if. . ." is a helpful way to encourage him to think out his actions when I am not home.

Betsy Ames Northport, NY

When my children were about 3, I started letting them play outside alone, but I never left the window for more than a few seconds! I would lay down certain rules: "Stay away from the gates," "Stay where I can see you," and "Don't talk to anyone you don't know and love." When I saw they were obeying all rules, I trusted them more.

Janet Bauer Islip Terrace, NY

At 2½, he could play in our backyard alone, but since we're in a town house the yard is very small: every corner visible from the kitchen. At 3, we're starting to let him ride his Big Wheel out on our court after lots of discussions of limits and appropriate behavior.

Lisa Mead Hughes Santa Clara, CA

When she understood about the dangers of getting lost, stranger danger, and to wait for Mom who will be right back.

P. Woods Ridgewood, NJ

My kids (6, 3) play alone outside in a fenced yard. We live on a busy street and they are never allowed anywhere except the back yard and even then I'm always watching.

Susan Barnett Waco, TX

When my oldest turned 8 I began letting him stay home alone or with one of the younger children for very short periods. He is 9 now and I think the longest I've left him is an hour.

Jill Heasley Fresno, CA

I allowed my son to play outside on the driveway at 4½, on the sidewalk at 5½, and on the street at 6½. I'd like to keep him near me until he's 13, but he won't let me. My almost 4 was playing on the driveway last summer but I was at the door checking every 2 minutes.

Maryann Shutan Highland Park, IL

I let my daughter play outside alone at age 4! The street was a dead end and we have a huge backyard. I feel comfortable if my 2-year-old is with big sister as our yard is fenced in.

Kathy Lord Rochester, MN

If they understand safety and strangers they are ready. Our daughter, 4, was careful and cautious. However, our son at 5 is enough to give me gray hairs! He'd believe anyone about anything. It truly depends on the child's development.

Kris Gialdini Fremont, CA

This depends solely on the maturity of your child. Some can be trusted at 2, others seem to be more inquisitive about life and are always into mischief regardless of their age.

Dolores DalSanto Florence, WI

At 3, my son only played outside when my husband or I were with him. The summer he turned 4, I could hardly keep him inside. At first I let him play only in the backyard (fenced in) and I kept my eye on him as much as possible. It wasn't long though, before he wanted to be in front. After Eric met some children he would start inching down the street. By the end of summer I was letting him go to their house. My husband thinks I'm too free with him, but he just loves to be outdoors when it's warm.

Kathy Brockman Sidney, OH

My son plays outside alone and has ever since he quit eating and putting everything into his mouth. When he is outside playing he comes inside approximately every 5 to 10 minutes to let me know what he is doing. He is never really alone, and neither am I!

Pam Stuart Tulsa, OK

A mother knows through intuition when they are ready. To help the transition of being left home alone: 1. make sure your child can dial a phone, 2. make sure rules about not letting in strangers are understood and how to handle phone calls when you're not there, and *most importantly*, 3. always leave a note saying where you will be, what time you'll be home and how to be reached.

Agnes Ferguson Ann Arbor, MI

3 years old. He insists on being outside (We live on a farm in rural Georgia) and at times I can't be. I'm not always comfortable with that.

Catherine Amos Cunning, GA

parents forum paren

Q How do you make the transition from worker to parent?

At first it was very hard; I felt I had to be "Super-Mom." I realized I couldn't be, and now I just try my best. When I come home, my son gets my undivided attention until his excitement wears off. I have learned one important thing: you can't let the "working mother guilties" prevent you from giving the discipline with love, when you're home.

C. Edwards, Hazel Park, MI

The best way I know is to have a husband who is a FULL participant in childrearing. I happen to love to cook, and my "get it together" time is having enough peace to cook a good dinner for us all. My husband and son play outside or go to the local play lot; in winter they read or play a game. We eat late, but we're used to it and enjoy the routine.

Christine O'Neill, Chicago, IL

Before I pick up our little girl at her regular sitter's, I take a few minutes for myself — run some errands, go to a garage sale, visit a friend or just window shop.

Kay Nelson, Long Lake, MN

I never thought of it as a problem. I'm always happy to get home, and the kids are happy to see me.

Katherine Z. Walker, Bradford, VT

We take time to talk and listen to our children for the first 20 to 30 minutes we are home. We take turns cleaning up after dinner. One of us spends time in the kitchen, the other in the living room. If I'm alone, the dishes usually wait until the kids are in bed. My husband helps a great deal; we both teach, so he realizes that the home work needs to be shared.

Sandra Kushner, Bliss, NY

How I wish I had the answer! After two years of being back at work, I still find the transition hard, sometimes suffocating, and only compounded by having to be sympathetic wife at the same time. I must be doing something wrong!

Barbara Ness, Hammonton, NJ

To avoid the rush of the evening meal, I prepare everything for it the night before. Then we all take a 30-minute walk while it cooks in the oven or microwave. It's great after sitting at a desk all day and conducive to family discussion.

Michelle Sheehy, Roseville, MN

My three rules for the transition are: (1) leave work at work; (2) remember the adage, "A clean house is a sign of a life misspent;" and (3) remind myself of the pledge I made myself 14 months ago that quality time is more important than quantity time in mothering.

Carol Phares, Breckenridge, MO

It's easy — I'm a mother first, then a teacher. I'm also fortunate that my babysitter does some of my cleaning and washing. When I come home we get supper started and sit down to read or play until it's ready. We're anxious to see each other after a day apart.

Deborah Grubb, Hebron, ND

It was easy for me, because I missed my son. I was ready to become Mom again when I came home. What I didn't manage to do well was to be an instant homemaker and cook. Mom was easy — Cook was not.

Ruth Genschoreck, Downers Grove, IL

I never did handle it well. I had my own seasonal business for six months of the year (plus all weekends of the year). When the baby came (after three older ones), I knew what I was missing and had missed, so I quit. I WISH I had not hollered about undone chores and had sat on the couch with them when I walked in. My energy was limited; I was overwhelmed. I'm glad to be home now.

Merrie Ann Handley, Boulder Creek, CA

Still, I envy you not having to go to work every day, Ellen...

from *Do They Ever Grow Up* by Lynn Johnston

I have a half-hour drive home from work, which allows me to unwind. Then I give myself about 15 minutes with my daughter to talk, cuddle, laugh and share each other's day before tackling supper.

Jane Wegner, Grafton, WI

If your children are home alone for part of the day, think seriously about:
- FIRE. No cooking, until you're sure they're old enough; no snacks that need heating; no playing with matches. A well-rehearsed fire drill gives them protection and you peace of mind.
- INTRUSION. No opening of doors to strangers or delivery men (parcels can be left outside the door). Tell the kids to call you, or a neighbor, if anyone tries persistently to get in.
- GUNS. Banish them! Gun accidents cause 1,200 deaths a year, over 10,000 injuries.
- PHONE CALLS. Teach your children to avoid telling callers that you're not home. If it's easier for them, keep a written message handy for them to read: "My mother can't take your call right now. Give me your number, and she'll call back as soon as possible."

forum parents forum

After a particularly hectic day, I linger for just a few moments in my car or at my desk. I stretch my whole body, scratch my scalp and shake my head, to wake up and feel more relaxed. Then I try to push all thoughts of work out of my mind. If I've had an extremely tiring day, I plan for an easy-meal, no-housework night. I try especially to relax and enjoy my kids; they can really pick up on your tiredness and distraction. It's truly easier to join them in their simple happy ways than to try to shut them out and worry about the office.

Cynthia Sato, Lansing, MI

I started working again four months ago; my son is 2. I found it extremely hard to relax once I got home — I rushed to get dinner, do the washing and tidy up, and naturally, he wanted my attention. After a few unnerving weeks, I realized I had to come home, relax, enjoy my son and worry about the housework later.

Cynthia Randi, Saratogo, WY

I have an arrangement with my sitter to pick up the children an hour after I leave work. I go home and change clothes (I work in military uniform), run errands or do dishes, so that I have at least an hour of free time to give the children when I pick them up.

Marcie Chamberlain, Roosevelt Roads, PR

I pick up my son at a daycare center. The time spent driving home is his to share the exciting news of the day. While driving, I also make an "appointment" to spend some time with him later in the evening. When we arrive home, he chooses an activity in his room until dinner. I relax, look at the mail or read the paper. Later, we use the "appointment time" to look at his school papers, read together and so on. My son's now 8; we've enjoyed this routine since he was 5.

Diana Hestwood, Minneapolis, MN

I spend 10 or 15 minutes with my son, playing outside or reading a book, before starting dinner.

Rebecca Kajander, Wayzata, MN

If you've had a bad day, try to leave it at the office. My limited time with my daughter (2½) is too valuable to deprive her and myself when my mind is elsewhere. Trying to cook dinner, clean house and wash clothes between quitting time and bedtime is difficult, but since it must be done I try to include her in my activities, by having her help. I spend time with her, and she is learning responsibility and independence. I wouldn't trade these times for anything.

Denica Mueffelman, Wayzata, MN

___

TWO CAN LIVE AS CHEAPLY AS ONE — IF THEY BOTH HAVE GOOD JOBS

I go to school, rather than work, so I have the same problem. So far I'm handling it by ignoring both kids (7½ and 4½) until I feel somewhat relaxed. They have things to do alone, and I encourage them. Later I try to have a time alone with each and some time together, too.

Frances Putnam, San Diego, CA

Grit my teeth and forge ahead! When you have to do it, even when you'd prefer going into a coma, what other way is there?

Mary Schultz, Rochester, MN

My mother had a quiet period for herself, to rest (when we were older, 12 and up), before we bothered her. When we were younger, I guess she just weathered the storm.

Lara Hengstebeck, Dearborn, MI

I worked with my first and a short while with the second. I loved the warm feeling that they still wanted me to be their Mom as soon as I got there.

Nancee Teresi, Santa Cruz, CA

It was so awful I quit work — and there was only one, then.

Cynthia Orloff, Detroit, MI

___

The "Working" Mom: I'll Drink to That!

"Are you a working mother?" the voice at the other end of the telephone inquired.

Frankly, I always thought that *all* mothers were working mothers. But I knew what she meant — was I one of those who toiled Out There to gain fulfillment, a pay check and a twenty-two hour day?

Not so far, I'm not. But the thought crosses my mind every so often. (Actually, it crosses my mind every afternoon about three-thirty as the kids pile in the door.)

I have to admit that the prospect of earning some extra cash does sound thrilling. So that is why, a few weeks ago, I scanned the want ads with rising hopes. Surely there must be — somewhere — the Perfect Situation for me. But there was no Perfect Situation available. I found several jobs for which I was eminently well qualified, but being a shortorder cook, school bus driver, hygiene inspector or maintenance maid

fell short of the dream role I had envisioned.

When I told my husband this, my latest failing, he looked up from the editorial page in astonishment. "Look for a job?" he gasped. "You can't be serious! Why, if you weren't here, this place would collapse into decay and ruin!"

I glanced around at the quite-obvious decay and ruin.

"I can't understand why you'd bother looking for the Perfect Situation," he went on, "when it's right here under your nose."

At this point, I retired to the kitchen to hunt for a box of crying tissues and a bottle of wine.

By Joan Wester Anderson

These are just a few of the very delightful, witty tidbits about child-coping and family life from Anderson's and Ann Toland Serb's book, STOP THE WORLD . . . OUR GERBILS ARE LOOSE!

 parents forum

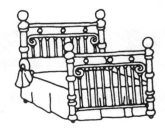

Q How do you feel about kids sleeping with you in your bed?

Your "pros" outweighed your "cons" by a good bit. Among PP readers, at least, it seems that the old-wives tales about co-family sleeping being "wrong" are outdated. Most of you who said "NO" cited lack of space or children's physical activity, not the possibility of deep psychological problems, as their reason.

I saw Tine Thevenin, author of THE FAMILY BED, on the Phil Donahue show—she was magnificent! For years my children (the oldest is 8) have slept with us intermittently. We weren't aware of the cultural taboos of co-family sleeping and I never felt it was "wrong" until I listened to other mothers.

As a working mother, I had two objectives: to get enough rest at night so I could be cheerful and in top form during the day and to raise a loving and secure child. One of the ways I coped with the guilt feelings about being away during the day was to snuggle a warm little body at night. (I still found plenty of time to snuggle my husband's warm big body, too. Dark nights and beds are not the only places for sex and loving—GOOD, but not too imaginative!)

The whole thing boils down to individual taste. If you and your husband feel comfortable with the arrangement, tell Dr. Spock or whoever to go butt a stump!

Gilda Henderson, Corpus Christi, TX

Ed. note: THE FAMILY BED can be ordered directly from Tine Thevenin at P.O. Box 16004, Minneapolis, MN 55416 for $8.95ppd

We shared a bed with our daughter on a vacation, when she was 18 months old. None of us got our proper sleep. When we returned home she could not wait to get into her own bed. Neither could my husband and I.

Helen Snelgrove, W. Bloomfield, MI

At infant and toddler stage, for comforting and such, that's fine. But neither my husband nor I encourage it. Our son has been in his own room since 3 weeks of age and seems none the worse for it. Both parents and children need privacy and spaces of their own.

Patrice Byron, Long Branch, NJ

It's best not to get them in the habit, as it is hard to break. But I guess it's better than having them wander from bed to bed in the middle of the night—or having them sleep on the floor, where it's drafty.

Bessie Dobbs, Lakeville, MN

It's the most natural thing in the world! I'm Chinese and my husband is Jamaican and we were both brought up sleeping with our parents. He was known as "poor," not "spoiled." In our culture, the kids who have their own beds (not to mention bedrooms) are the ones who are "spoiled." We push two double beds together and put on those marvelous bed sacks so we don't have to deal with bedspreads.

Connie Tenn, West Linn, OR

Adults sleep together and put a new baby, who's been in a warm, moist womb for nine months, into a cold crib all alone. How utterly insane! Dr. Herbert Ranter of Chicago says if you answer your child's needs now, when he's older he won't be on your doorstep. Also, your child won't feel the need for security as a teenager and won't be sleeping around.

Carlene Parsons, Ellsworth, ME

I couldn't figure out how to make our king-sized bed fit us all in. A friend told me she took one of the sides off the crib and scooted it right up to the bed. It worked perfectly. Admittedly, my husband was never really sold on the idea (didn't like sleeping with a little foot in his back or a little hand massaging his head), but after the kids moved to their own room he said he missed that special closeness. It is really true that our children TOUCH a lot more than others.

A friend of mine found HER perfect solution—she turns rock and roll music on the transistor radio in the baby's room, hands him a bottle and shuts the door. It might be easier and less hassle, but in my mind it is dangerous, damaging and non-caring.

Linda Trust, Riverside, CA

If it's okay for them to sit on your lap during the day, their need for closeness doesn't end because it's nighttime. I don't encourage it, but I don't deny them, either. I think the idea that it will make them have sexual ideas is crazy, when they're little. If they are 8 or 10 or so, that's different.

Joyce Jacobsen, St. Edward, NB

"Experts," Pro and Con

John Rosemond is one author who's not in favor of the family bed. In his syndicated column, "Parents," he recently wrote:

"When a child is put to bed lovingly but authoritatively by parents who insist he stay there until morning, he learns that separation from them is not the horrible thing he imagined. The way bedtime is handled sets a precedent for other separation experiences, such as leaving the child with a sitter, taking him to daycare and sending him off to school. A child who learns to separate easily at bedtime will have a much easier time with other separations as well. He will be more trusting of his parents and therefore more capable of exercising his potential for independence."

Tine Thevenin feels differently about independence. "A child who has his needs fulfilled will become an independent person," she writes in THE FAMILY BED. "But independence cannot be forced upon someone. It takes time and growing at the individual's own pace. The more secure he is in the knowledge that he can always come back to his parents, the more independent he will become. We only create problems if we regard his needing us at night as a problem which should be 'cured.' "

I can never believe it when I hear about people sleeping with their kids! We tried it with our toddler when he woke at night and it was great if you like drool on your pillow and being kicked in the back constantly. His favorite is to say, "Eye" and stick his finger in your eye. Can people really get any sleep with little kids?

Priss Baker, Aurora, CO

There are disadvantages: sleeping "on the alert" so as not to roll over on your 3-month-old, not being able to have complete freedom of movement in bed and having to change our sheets more often because his diapers usually leak. Also, it has put a damper on our love life. But both my husband and I think it's worth it. I think, having followed our instincts thus far, we'll continue to let him sleep with us until those same instincts tell us not to.

Georgia Walsh, Alexandria, VA

parentsforum

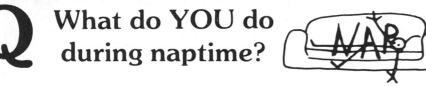

Q What do YOU do during naptime?

First, I leap about, cheering. Then I clean one room and sit there.

A. Hurst, Ottawa, Ont.

When my infant took naps, I stared blankly out the window and thought about the days before he was born! I also tried to look ahead at the positive changes of my life in the hope that I could relax long enough to catnap. I always viewed this time as MINE and didn't do anything that involved "work."

Helen Lazar, Orange Village, OH

Unfortunately, my kids rarely nap at the same time. I usually end up spending some special time with whichever one is awake. I enjoy this, but on those rare days I have an hour alone it sure is a big treat.

Tina Rohde, Eden Prairie, MN

Sleep, eat, read or be merry with my hubby—afternoon delight!

Karen Bergher, Anaheim, CA

When they napped, I used to read and nap at the same time. When they stopped napping, it was like quitting smoking again for me to give up my nappy time.

Kathy Hickok, Delray Beach, FL

Sneak my diet soda first thing. Three days out of five, I usually do chores; one day, paperwork (answer your survey, pay bills, etc.); and one day I collapse and read. On weekends, I may get a haircut or do errands, since my husband's home.

Gene Storz, Denver, CO

I read, study, write letters, occasionally nap myself—but NEVER housework. My husband shares that, so I never feel a need to do any during naptime. We all work on it together in the evening. That one to two hours every afternoon keeps me sane!

Unsigned

I take a shower and groom myself, adding lotion to my face and skin, grooming my eyebrows and nails while my 4-year-old listens to records or plays. If there is time leftover, I spend it with him, playing a game like Candyland before the baby is up.

Elsa Koosha, Endwell, NY

Right now, I have enough accumulated to last me a lifetime of naptimes! About all I can do is make lists of what to do when my extremely active 21-month-old is in bed and look at his 4-year-old sister to remind myself that they DO grow up.

Unsigned

NAP! (Providing both kids nap at the same time, the doorbell doesn't ring, the Avon lady doesn't come, the washer doesn't throw itself off balance, the dryer buzzer doesn't go off, the dishwasher doesn't flood the kitchen, I don't break my neck falling over toys on the way to the bedroom, the boss isn't coming to dinner AND a telephone solicitor doesn't call trying to waterproof the basement I don't have.)

Jan Schmitz, St. Louis, MO

I take the phone off the hook, shut the front door so the neighbor kids don't disturb me—and swing into action. I clean the bathrooms or any other part of the house that is hard to clean with kids around, empty the dishwasher and clothes dryer, freeze or can in season. Very seldom do I nap. My time to relax is at night when the kids are in bed, and even then I find myself doing "just one more thing."

Corinne Powell, Dyer, IN

Sometimes I read my Bible or sew or study, since I am in college. It gives me time to breathe and reflect on many things in my life, and to me it's my "special time."

Romaine Doster, Washington, DC

Read PRACTICAL PARENTING! Naptime is Mom's time, so I do usually catch up on my reading or just take a "breather."

Gail Goldberg, Northridge, CA

THE AMOUNT OF SLEEP RE-QUIRED BY THE AVERAGE PERSON IS USUALLY 10 MINUTES MORE.

Have a cup of coffee, sit down and watch my SOAP!

Phyllis Stade, Mankato, MN

Ed. note: It wasn't part of the question, but it's interesting to note that any reader who named a "soap" she watches said "General Hospital."

Try to get my children to nap! It usually works best if they fall asleep in the car and I carry them in to their beds. Then, if they stay asleep, I get on my hands and knees and scrub the kitchen floor. It doesn't happen often, so if it weren't for our dog, we'd have a pretty dirty kitchen floor!

Margaret Cellette, St. Paul, MN

A cup of tea, Carly Simon on stereo, and then I SEW, SEW, SEW. That's MY time. Time for me! Just me! Tra-la! (And God help any interruptions!)

Judith Hudson, Cranston, RI

Usually I feel GUILTY because my 2-year-old naps during the only time during the day that both her older sisters are in school and I COULD spend time alone with her. But, guilty or not, I usually spend the time doing one of a million things I like to do, but not if kids are around.

Sandi Mink, Detroit, MI

ENJOY IT!

Barbara Sattora, Ruch, NY

And Then There Are Those Who . . .

. . . get more done than I do the rest of the day . . . escape to the solitude of lawn work . . . chat (uninterrupted!) on the phone . . . do needlepoint or embroidery . . . pursue a craft or hobby . . . write letters . . . go to the bathroom alone . . . exercise . . . tiptoe about, afraid to wake the baby . . . take off my shoes and get my feet up . . . eat lunch . . . do the paperwork for a home business . . . knit or crochet . . . pay the bills . . . do anything I can do lying down . . . meditate . . . or COLLAPSE!

parents forum

Q How do you leave a crying child with a sitter?

Most parents — but not all — are opposed to sneaking out after the sitter gets the child involved in something. Leavetaking "rituals" are developed by some: spending a few minutes playing or talking with the child, kissing and hugging, waving goodbye from the window, honking the car horn. And if you're leaving your child at a sitter's house, remember to bring a "talisman" from home — a blanket or a favorite toy or book.

We are going through a separation problem for the second time with our 14-month-old. I never sneak away; I always give her a kiss and tell her Mommy will come back. When I return, I repeat that Mommy always comes back. I'm told she only cries for a few minutes and then has a good time.
Linda Haugen, St. Paul, MN

Our daughter wanted very much to go to nursery school, but was terrified at first. I left her, crying, for a couple of days, but it only got worse. Then I spent two days at school with her, then just the first hour for a couple of days. It worked! After a week of her willing attendance, I tried joining a carpool — and was back at square one. She was afraid of riding in strange cars. So I drove the carpool daily for three weeks to get her used to riding with the other kids. From then on she's ridden happily with all the parents. I'm glad I took the time to work things out with her, though for awhile I wondered if it was worth it.
K. Ziegler-Walker, Bradford, VT.

Get down to eye-level with the child, explain what he or she will be doing, get the sitter or nursery school teacher involved. Say that it's important to you that his or her work or play is well done, so you can see it when you return. Most important, don't say you'll be back in "two hours;" that's scary. Talk in terms of activities, "after snack time," "after nap time."
Mary Ann Domzalski, Detroit, MI

A good prevention technique is to forewarn. Before I go, even days before, I let my daughter in on the fact that I'll be going. It seems to make a difference.
Mrs. Bob Koehs, Marquette, MI

from *Do They Ever Grow Up* by Lynn Johnston

I silently pray that I can be stronger than my child and not turn around as I leave. It's heart-wrenching, but they go through stages of this. The first time it happened, I felt sooo guilty, but no longer!
P. Schubert, Upr. Montclair, NJ

A good idea I read about: kiss your child's palm and close his/her fingers into a fist. Tell him/her that after you've left and s/he feels the need of a kiss, there's one there, in hand, all ready.
Harriet Meehan, Santa Fe, NM

I have only left my 2-year-old twice. Once she is interested in something or someone, I slip out. I feel sneaky, but it works.
Katie Brittain, Coleridge, NC

I was lucky, in that my son cried very little when I left. In fact, I was devastated on my son's first day of nursery school when he simply looked at me and said, "'Bye, mom," and went back to playing.
Debbie Purcell, Syracuse, NY

Seeking Sitters

Once upon a time, there were grandparents, aunts, sisters and cousins who seemed to like nothing better than to care for babies and children. Not so, today, for most parents. Oh, there are some lucky ones who have access to a relative or two, but most, unless they work out "trades" with friends or belong to baby-sitting co-ops, have to depend on their own ingenuity (and some cash) to get sitters. To find reliable teen-agers and young adults, they:

• Talk with friends and neighbors who have or know boys and girls who sit.

• Call the home economics departments of nearby high schools or colleges to get names of young people who take family living classes and want practice.

• Contact YWCAs, Girl Scout Councils, Camp Fire Girls and parks and recreation departments, all of which may offer baby-sitting courses and have lists of willing applicants.

• Call local churches, which sometimes keep lists of young members who wish to sit.

In order to make super sitters of these boys and girls, the parents pay well (by the hour or the half-hour); tip for extra work or long hours; leave detailed, clear instructions; and treat sitters with respect and consideration, making them "members of the family." Often they ask a sitter for a get-acquainted visit, while they're home, before the first job.

Parents who want to find adult sitters:

• Put ads in the paper (and check out references carefully).

• Call on commercial sitting services found through the yellow pages.

• Make friends with neighboring middle-aged women who enjoy baby-sitting.

Dear Babysitter Handbook
This guide for your sitter has all the information needed while you are away. Included is basic first-aid, a medical release form and fill ins for important facts and more.

parents forum

Q How did you manage your maternity leave?

The Pregnancy Discrimination Act, which was passed in 1978, helped to clarify and liberalize corporate policy on maternity leave, and many companies now offer more paid disability leave to new mothers and more unpaid leave to both parents. According to a study of 1500 major corporations conducted by the Catalyst Career and Family Center in New York, most women do not take lengthy maternity leaves. A majority (63%) of new mothers take five to eight weeks off after the birth of a child.

The hospital where I work offers 50 paid sick days per year with a doctor's note. I managed to stay well during my pregnancy and I worked until two days before my son was born. I took the remaining 48 days off as maternity leave. I felt pretty awful the last month that I worked and for the first two or three months when I returned. I really wish I could have taken six months off.
Denise Hultz Detroit, MI

I had a six-week leave, but it wasn't long enough. We were only just getting adjusted. I was lucky, however, because I received permission to take my daughter to work with me until she was 9 months old. I wouldn't have traded that for anything. I needed to work, and I needed to be with my daughter. I was the director of an after-care program for adults who have been institutionalized, so it was easy to have a baby along. Maybe this experience is part of the reason that my daughter (now 6) is so independent and adjusts easily to new and different situations.
Sandy Batson Morgantown, WV

I took nine months of leave from my full-time job. After sick leave, vacation, and disability ran out, we lived on my husband's salary for five months. I saved every penny I could during my pregnancy to have this extra time with my son. Our budget was tight. With a supporting husband and an employer who helped me make arrangements, I now job share a position. This involved taking a lower salary. All the struggles have been very rewarding. They grow so fast!
Mary Enriquez Santee, CA

I took two months off, and everything worked out well. I'm very thankful for that time. I was originally going to take only two weeks—it would have been nuts!! I was replaced by a school teacher who was off for the summer. Maybe women who are expecting during those months could consider teachers as possible replacements.
Lynne Shortridge-Tornell Phoenix, AZ

I arranged an open-ended leave with an understanding boss. I told him I would most likely return part-time at six months. I was ready at five months, but couldn't find a satisfactory day-care mom, so I ended up going back at six months as planned. I realize how fortunate I am to have had the flexibility. My advice: look for day care early!
C. Waddington Seattle, WA

I took a three-month leave and then worked half-time until Brennan was 6 months old. At that point I was to go back full time, but I realized that would be too much. Thanks to a patient and supportive boss, I cut my hours to 30. By the time Brennan was a year old, though, I decided even 30 hours was too much. My life was too hectic and I wasn't functioning well either at home or at work. I quit and now I'm home full time. It's a temporary retirement from my career, and it has been a hard adjustment, but having more time with Brennan (now 19 months old) is wonderful.
Leeanne Mallonee Bangor, ME

I had six weeks of unpaid leave. I returned to work part time and gradually increased my hours back to full time at ten months. I'm a high level manager and my job has some flexibility, which helps.
Bobbie Baker Seattle, WA

I took a three month leave. It should have been three years! My son is 5 now. When he was 3 I was able to quit working away from home. I did not know that maternal love would be so strong.
Barbara Balascio Dayton, OH

I had three months of disability leave. I was not ready physically or emotionally to go back until the baby was 4 months old. For that fourth month we lived on credit cards. I'm tired, but I'm glad I get to spend days with my child (now 13 months) and work evenings.
Lynn Mechanic San Francisco, CA

Mother Care/Other Care

Employment outside the home is either a choice or a necessity for a majority of mothers with preschool children. More than six million American families face the dilemma of what to do with their children during working hours. The decision can be baffling, traumatic, and guilt-inducing.

Child development psychologist Dr. Sandra Scarr has written a book about the problems these working parents must face. Her book, *Mother Care/Other Care* (Basic Books, 1984, $16.95) demonstrates that good child care takes many forms and that round-the-clock parental presence is not essential for the development of a normal, healthy child.

Here are some of the reassuring points Dr. Scarr makes in her book:

- Day care (if carefully chosen) is not bad for young children; in fact, it has many benefits.

- Placing an infant under six months of age in day care will cause the *least* upset to the baby. A baby's attachment to someone other than its mother does not interfere with the mother/child relationship. Babies in day care still turn to their mothers for primary emotional support.

- Working mothers spend just as much time interacting with their children as do mothers who do not work outside the home.

- There is no significant difference in school achievement, IQ scores, and social development between children of working and non-working mothers.

I requested four months part-time work, which was accomplished through job sharing. New York State allows six weeks of maternity leave, which is insufficient and borderline antihumanitarian. I received half pay during my leave which, luckily, was extended because of prolonged bleeding!
Unsigned

I arranged a three-month leave, but when my twins arrived prematurely, I finally gave up the idea (painfully) of continuing my career. After 4½ years of being a full-time mother, though, I'm very happy to have been home with my children. They do go to school sometime—don't they??
Diana Wampole Allentown, PA

parentsforum

Q How do you coordinate nursing with a career?

I have successfully breastfed my two children and worked full-time. During three months of maternity leave, I gradually introduced a bottle during the day, one feeding at a time. I breastfeed when I return from work at 5, at night, and in the morning before I leave.

Becky Adams   Washington, DC

I went to school while nursing my youngest. I did my best to schedule around her, but it wasn't always possible. I relied heavily on my husband. One night when I came home late I found him giving her breast milk from a shot glass! It worked!

Nedra O'Neill   Evergreen Park, IL

I teach, and I hired an elderly lady to keep my son in an empty classroom. My breaks coincided with his schedule, so we continued breastfeeding without any problems. It helps to have cooperative administrators!

Judy Van Gorkom   Manteca, CA

I started back to work part-time when the baby was almost 2 months old. About a week before I went back, I cut out one feeding in what was to be the middle of my shift. Right before I'd leave for work, I would breastfeed. I would feel full by the end of the day, but usually I wouldn't have to pump. About three weeks later, I cut out another feeding. A month later, I eliminated another feeding. By the time the baby was six months old, I was down to one feeding every day or even every other day, and she didn't seem interested anymore. So I just stopped breastfeeding. I didn't feel a thing — she was weaned and so was I!

Jenifer Joy Madden   Arlington, VA

I went back to work when the baby was 8 weeks old. I would nurse her before work and pump twice a day at work. Her daycare center was close to work, so I nursed her there during my lunch hour. After 5 months, my milk supply decreased, so I supplemented one feeding at the daycare with formula. When she was 8 months old, I cut out the feedings one by one and weaned her. I'm so glad I attempted this. It isn't easy, but it is possible if you really want to.

An excellent breast pump is the Marshall pump, made in Japan.

Susan Erdman   Cincinnati, OH

I went back to work full-time when my son was 6 months old. I drove home *every* lunch hour to nurse, and pumped every two hours at work because of my huge milk supply. My son totally refused a bottle until I went to work. The first day of work he happily accepted a bottle. You figure it out!

Pia Parrish Lincoln   Ramona, CA

With great difficulty. My husband brought the baby to me between his classes or I met the babysitter at a daycare facility. The baby was not allowed on my work site. He was often hungry as he waited to be fed, and I had problems with leaking and engorgement.

Unsigned

Notes on Breastfeeding For Working Moms

What We Need to Hear

Working mothers spend as much time caring for their children as mothers who stay at home, according to a report issued by the National Research Council.

It seems that the most important indicator of a child's well-being is the child's social and economic environment. Two working parents provide more income and, with it, a greater sense of security and basic economic well-being, as well as more benefits and opportunities.

Children of satisfied mothers are better adjusted than those of discontented mothers, whether the mothers work outside of the home or not, the report concludes.

Minneapolis Star and Tribune, Oct. 28, '82

It's definitely demanding, but worth it! I work two full days and one half day. I expressed milk for my son until just recently. At 11 months, he nurses in the morning and even before bed. He drinks regular milk during the day and does great! I really respect working mothers who give up their lunch hours and breaks for breastfeeding.

Mary Enriquez   Santee, CA

I used my break to express milk, which then went in the freezer. Between that and expressing first thing in the morning (once he slept through), he only needed about eight ounces of formula a week. Breast pumps never worked for me. I taught myself to express manually by nursing him on my right side, holding a bottle in my right hand, with my right arm supporting him, and expressing milk with my left hand. Very awkward, but his nursing got my let-down reflex going and I learned how to express.

Lisa Mead Hughes   Santa Clara, CA

My neighbor, who was nursing her own baby, nursed mine for me when she took care of her.

Lynn Mechanic   San Francisco, CA

The children's babysitter lives one block from the school where I teach, so I could go there and breastfeed. My daughter was breastfed until 20 months. My 22-month-old son is still nursing. How nice to spend my lunch hour with my feet up, nursing and cuddling the kids! I remember worrying that I'd be too frazzled after school to nurse. What a pleasant surprise to find that nursing relaxed me and helped me thoroughly enjoy that time of day with my children!

Barb Ingalsbe   Norfolk, NE

I returned to night work (11-7) after a 2½ month maternity leave. I feed the baby right before I go, then put her down for the night. She usually sleeps all night and I feed her when I get home. I pump my breasts at 2:30 a.m. wheather or not it's a work night and freeze the milk for possible use later. Pumping regularly keeps me on a schedule. So far this has kept the milk coming in nicely.

Anne Moller   Woodinville, WA

I went back to work when my daughter was 9 months old. The caregiver gave her bottles (expressed milk or formula). I enjoyed sitting down and nursing as soon as I got home. I nursed evenings and weekends. I did not express milk at work. The supply just seemed to adjust to what was needed at different times. I continued nursing until my daughter was 4 years old! I'm a firm believer that you don't have to wean when you go back to work!

Claudia Tolar   Running Springs, CA

I nursed only first thing in the morning and last thing at night. It was best for me physically and emotionally. It kept us close but relieved the pressure to be Supermom.

Unsigned

parentsforum

Q What eating habits have you passed on to your kids?

Like most semi-liberal raised-in-the-60s people, I had visions of a super-healthy granola-eating child who broke out in hives at the sight of junk food. There's one thing I didn't count on: my husband, the potato chip and Pepsi king of the free world. By 18 months, my daughter's vocabulary included Pepsi, chippies, and chocolate cake. To say the least, I was discouraged. But I didn't give up, and my efforts were rewarded to a degree. She still likes junk food, but she prefers fruit to candy, and cheese to chocolate cake. My advice: don't give up on nutrition.

Tere Turner Cameron, NC

We only eat healthy food in our home. We avoid sugary and sweetened food for the most part and eat nothing that has been prepared with artificial ingredients, preservatives, or additives. Bodies are natural; why add anything unnatural to them? The other positive influence is giving him water instead of gallons of juice, which is so sweet even if it is "natural." If he snacks, it's on carrots, cheeses, and other good food.

Debbie Hoffman Plotkin San Diego, CA

I have a sweet tooth and love to bake, but my children would rather have fruit. Good kids!

Blythe Lipman Millville, NJ

I hate milk and my little girl won't drink it either.

Lisa Smith Hurst, TX

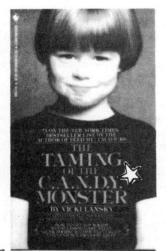

☆ Continuously, Advertised, Nutritionally, Deficient, Yummies!

Being an avid weight watcher, I've managed to avoid giving Michael (2½) snacks and junk food all day long. This had a bad side effect, however. When he goes to a friend's house where they serve a lot of treats, he eats them like they're going out of style!

Jeri Wilkes W. Jordan, UT

Since I won't touch any type of seafood, I've never offered it to my kids. Unfortunately, I've created an aversion to this healthy food as a result. And I've never even *tasted* seafood!

Myra Weaver Hollywood, FL

I worry about my daughter who at 7 is like a stick and claims she's fat. I wonder if she's headed for anorexia nervosa in her teens. My husband claims she's mimicking me. I'm 5'1", and every ounce looks like a pound on me. I have to watch *every* bite.

Jerri Oyama Northridge, CA

I'm a health-food nut. I sneak yogurt, fresh fruit, sunflower seeds, Brewer's yeast, etc., into their diet. I've been doing this since they were babies. It's a struggle because they *love* junk food.

Leigh Galey Metairie, LA

Overeating! My son is not overweight at all, but I think he would be if he were more sedentary. He eats a lot, but he burns it off. Not the same for Mom unluckily!

Kris Taranec Lake Havasu, AZ

My husband and I eat *anything!* Our three children are so picky it's disgusting. I always heard if your children saw you eat something, they would too. That hasn't worked at our house!

Mary Ellen Cooper Glendale, AZ

My daughter (6) understands what foods are good and what is junk. She knows to eat just a little sugar and she knows what foods have sugar. I was a fat child. My daughter is of average size. She understands that people get fat because they eat when they aren't hungry. My eating habits have improved over the years and my daughter benefits from that.

Karen Haynes Upper Marlboro, MD

I have changed my eating habits dramatically to set an example for my child. We have lots of vegetables and fruit and quality protein items now instead of the fast food and junk I used to eat. My son eats well and is concerned about nutrition in spite of the influence of his friends. I expect the big challenge to come after he goes to school.

Unsigned

I prefer fruit to candy, cake, and ice cream and I have tried to instill that same preference in my daughter. It's very hard when TV commercials promote cookies, ice cream, candy, etc. every time you turn around.

Anne Schuster St. Paul, MN

Would you believe wheat germ? My daughter (22 mos.) saw me eating it straight from the jar and wanted to try it. Now she loves it (straight from the jar, of course).

Donna Poplawski Houghton, MI

If I don't want my children to eat something, I just don't buy it.

Lynn Hall Fort Lauderdale, FL

Say Yes to Less

Spring is a good time to re-evaluate our eating habits and shape up for summer. Now is the time to shed excess winter pounds and become more aware of the food we are serving our families. We can all benefit by reducing the amounts of fat, salt, and sugar that we consume.

Less fat—Buy leaner ground beef in bulk to offset the higher cost, trim fat from meat before cooking, limit fried foods, use butter and margarine in moderation, and limit lunch meats and sausage-type products.

Less salt—Do not salt meat before cooking (it promotes shrinkage); season food in the kitchen and discourage salting at the table; use onion, parsley, chives, garlic, and other herbs and spices instead of salt; limit cured meats.

Less sugar—Use sugar in moderation. For most recipes, the sugar can be reduced by one third without affecting the flavor; encourage snacking on fresh fruit rather than cookies or candy. Use unsweetened or lightly sweetened beverages instead of soda. Restrict artificially sweetened beverages, especially for children.

By settling for a little less, you will really be doing a lot more for you and your family!

Judy Beto, R.D. Pacesetter, May 1983

parentsforum

Q Has coaching kid's behavior backfired?

After my son finished performing in the church Christmas program, he returned to his seat by me and said in a *loud* whisper, "Aren't you proud of me? I didn't pick my nose!"

Susan Barnett   Waco, TX

My 6 year old had a habit of sucking her finger upon going to bed. She was developing a callous on her finger, so I told her the finger would fall off if she didn't stop. She ended up telling this to our pediatrician —who got quite a laugh out of it!

Sharon Beyer   Milwaukee, WI

Yes, and I don't do it anymore. I'm not worried about what Nick will say, because I'm honest and so is he. What's the need for coaching?

Kris Taranec   Lake Havasu City, AZ

In a way—try telling them *not* to talk about anything. "I've got a secret!"

Lisa Schickedanz   Gage, OK

I don't coach them and *that* has backfired. I can't believe what they repeat and say on their own. Our 4-year-old son said he knows why people shouldn't drink and drive—they might spill their drink!

Kris Gialdini   Fremont, CA

Are you kidding? What mother of a child older than 2 hasn't had the experience of having their child repeat *some* embarrassing instruction to a grown-up. "My mommy says you shouldn't pick your nose 'cause it isn't polite."

Pat Spiker   Columbus, OH

We have a little neighbor girl who likes to hit other kids. After trying different ways of dealing with it, we finally told our kids they could hit her back when she hits them. Not long after this, the little girl and our kids were playing and I heard a fight start. Then I heard my 4-year-old say, "Turn around, I have to hit your back." I quickly explained—after I stopped chuckling.

Donna Schreier   St. Paul, MN

Don't tell them what *not* to say—for they'll surely say it!

Pat Leask   Munster, Ont.

Our son shook hands and said, "Pleased to meet you," to an "important" adult, then added, "Momma said if I did that, I can have Cheerios for a snack."

Unsigned

Oh, yeah! If I do, I end up mouthing the sentence with them—not *very* discreet! They just feel too much "on the spot" and mess it up anyway. It's best to let them do it their way.

Maureen Deitsch   Toledo, OH

My kids' "wisecracking" and "innocent remarks" have embarrassed me many times. Now when I sense something coming, I tell them to keep all comments until we get back to the car.

Connie Tenn   West Linn, OR

Lindley refuses to be coached. He becomes stoically silent. However, he loves to play-act situations both before and after they occur.

Sarah Schiermayer   Weston, MA

No, because I don't coach my son on what to say except please and thank you. I feel children need to speak and say what's on their minds (within reason). Too many adults have trouble expressing themselves.

Jeri Wilkes   Puyallup, WA

I don't know why, but whenever I want my kids to thank someone (and I specifically ask them to) they always seem to resent it, and it shows in their attitude.

Agnes Ferguson   Ann Arbor, MI

He said TRUCK...didn't you, darling... He said truck!

from Do They Ever Grow Up by Lynn Johnston

Ten years ago, when I found out that I was pregnant for the first time, I decided that I was going to become the best parent I could be. I armed myself with loads of information. I decided I would meet each stage of childhood with the patience of a saint.

It was three and a half years and three children later, when my vision of being the "perfect parent" began to blur. How come not one of the books I had read prepared me for "Life's Most Embarrassing Moments"?

My first such moment was at a fast-food restaurant that serves chicken. I asked my children to tell me just how hungry they were so I would know what to order. They each told me they were so hungry that they could eat an astronomical number of chicken parts. I left them giggling in their seats under the watchful eye of the other patrons in the restaurant.

Somehow, however, they went from discussing chicken parts to discussing parts of the human body. Their admirers were smiling and remarking how wonderful it was that they were so informed about their bodies. Then, there was total silence interrupted only by the voice of my four-year-old daughter saying, "I'm so hungry, I could eat your penis." That was closely followed by my five-year-old son's words, "I'm so hungry I could eat your vagina." And then they innocently went on from there naming all the other parts of each other's bodies that they were planning on eating.

I grabbed the counter for fear of fainting. I turned around because I feared that I might have to perform CPR on the two older women seated behind my children. I slowly peeled my fingers from the counter, returned to my children, and choked down my lunch.

Besides chicken, I have choked on my own words on a few other occasions. Like the time my son of six years told me to close my eyes because he thought for sure *I* was about to get sick to my stomach. Naturally, he got my full attention, plus the attention of the other twenty or so people seated in our doctor's waiting room. I asked him what he meant by his statement. He pointed to the lady sitting across from him and said, "Remember when you said it made you sick when you saw a baby drinking a bottle full of soda?" He continued to tell me how this woman, whose nose was at the end of his finger, had just given such a bottle to the baby nestled in her arms!

Nedra O'Neill

parentsforum

Working Parents' Dilemma

Where can working parents turn when they have a sick child and there is no relative or trusted friend handy to babysit? More and more, parents are looking to employers for solutions. A recent study conducted by Parents in the Workplace (Minneapolis) concluded with the following recommendations:

- Corporations should provide guidance and counseling for working parents to explain absentee policies and sick child care alternatives.

- Sick child care alternatives should be made available by employers. Options should range from time off to care for a child during the acute phase of an illness or until other arrangements can be made, to in-home sick care services or sick care in a satellite family day care home or child care center.

- Innovative sick care programs such as in-home sick care services, satellite family day care homes, or sick care centers should be considered by corporations and foundations for funding.

- Corporations should subsidize sick child care through an employee cost-sharing plan. This could be done as part of a flex benefit program, salary reduction plan, or as a direct subsidy. Such funding could be treated as an employer business expense if used for the purpose of reducing absenteeism or turnover.

- A sick care licensing rule should be explored with the Departments of Health and Welfare.

As one manager put it, "Underlying the sick child care syndrome is a cultural bias that does not give credance to child rearing. Corporations need to come to grips with the social importance of supporting sick child care by actively helping the responsible worker who happens to have sick care problems—through the types of policies corporations set, through flex time, through comp time off, etc. We need to support creative programs and be a creative force to think through alternatives to the sick child care problem."

Q Who cares for your sick child when you can't?

If my husband or I can't stay with them, we don't go. Nothing is more important than caring for a sick child.
Karen Dockrey Burke, VA

My mother always wants to help. In fact, she takes care of my son when *I'm* sick! I'm extremely lucky to have her.
Linda Richardson Phoenix, AZ

Can't imagine having to leave a sick child. I am so happy I work at home.
Kathy Hickok Delray Beach, FL

Fortunately, my job is flexible enough to allow me to be home whenever I think it is necessary. An understanding employer helps.
Pia Parrish Lincoln Spring Valley, CA

When my kids are sick, I want to be with them. Not that they can't survive without me, I just want to be there for them.
Jill Heasley Fresno, CA

I envy people who have family in the area to help. I have no relatives around and I could never leave a sick child with a babysitter.
Myra Weaver Hollywood, FL

I don't go because there's nothing worse than being sick with someone you don't know.
Unsigned

The regular caregiver watches them unless it's really serious. If it is, my husband or I stay home.
Linda Schweyer Detroit, MI

If my son is not too sick, my mother stays with him. If he feels really bad and just wants Mommy, then I stay home from teaching.
Unsigned

Either my husband or Grandma and Grandpa. If the kids are seriously ill, I take the day off. No one is quite as nice as Mom to have around when you're ill.
Sharon Beyer Milwaukee, WI

We live 2,000 miles from any relatives, so our next-door neighbor cares for our son. I trust her implicitly, even if he's ill.
Bethany Elliott Moore San Diego, CA

We stay home if the kids are really sick. Who wants a stranger around when you feel rotten?
Pat Spiker Columbus, OH

My husband and I alternate. He's a lawyer, so his schedule is flexible enough to allow this.
Gail Meyers Minneapolis, MN

If I cannot stay home, my terrific mother-in-law usually steps in.
Linda Merry St. Louis Park, MN

Fortunately my work schedule is flexible. I don't think I would be working if I had to leave my sick children and go to work.
MaryEllen Cooper Glendale, AZ

The same people who watch them when they're not sick. Our usual sitter is capable of caring for a sick child. (If they can survive me, they can survive anyone!)
Barbara Sattora Rush, NY

Since my business is at home, it enables me to stay home and care for sick children and still work. I highly recommend it.
Deb Julius Brick, NJ

I just don't go. I call in sick or cancel. I'm first and most important a MOMMY.
Nancee Teres Santa Cruz, CA

A registered nurse from an agency. It's expensive, but it's the only way I have peace of mind.
Sarah Schiermeyer Weston, MA

That's one reason I resigned.
Melissa Arnett South Charleston, WV

parentsforum

GUILT

Q **What do you do when two small kids need attention— NOW?**

First of all, you can't lump closely-spaced children and multiples together—it's like comparing apples and oranges. Even children only nine months apart are at very different stages of development and need different types of attention. I've had four children under 5, which included new-born twins. Believe me, twins are NOT the same as two close together. (Parents of multiples easily become obsessed with equality!)
Karen Gromada, Cincinnati, OH

My daughters are 15 months apart, and I have run into this problem many times. I can usually pick up one and hold the hand of the other while the latter explains what's going on for her. It gets harder as they get older because of the old green-eyed monster, JEALOUSY.
Nedra O'Neill, Calumet Park, IL

If my husband is near, I scream, "HELP!"
Kathy Whitman, Eatonton, GA

ONE (18 months) demands all my attention, so I would never have another one, at least for six or seven years. (I'm glad I didn't have twins!)
Michelle Medvedeff, Philadelphia, PA

If both my children need my attention right now, I just take a second to evaluate which is the most important. For example, if my 3½-year-old needs help getting dressed and my 21-month-old is about to smear peanut butter and jelly all over the furniture, the peanut butter and jelly wins, hands down. If one were hanging out the second story window and the other were headed for the street, I think I'd take care of whichever was closest first . . . and pray.
Valerie Cook, SugarLand, TX

I learned while helping in the church nursery on a busy Sunday that by sitting on the floor Indian style you can straddle a child on each leg and rock them against your body. If necessary, you can even hold one more child in the center.
Mrs. William Simmons, Springfield, VA

We adopted a baby girl and I gave birth to a boy eight months later. Although we were delighted, the first two years weren't easy. I don't know whether I ever really solved the problem of both needing my attention RIGHT NOW, but we did survive those years. I tried to take care of the one with the most pressing need first, but sometimes that wasn't easy to tell. I also let housework and a lot of other things take a back seat for awhile and lowered my standards in some ways. For example, I changed diapers when they were dripping, not just damp. Breastfeeding the younger one seemed to help, because I had one hand free to hold or hug the older one and I didn't have to waste time mixing formula and sterilizing bottles. It also helped to have an understanding husband.
Linda Brunn, Denver, CO

Immobilize one (crib, playpen, etc.) and deal with the other.
Jill Miller, Portland, OR

I get a lot of double demands, with boys 2 and 3. Usually I am able to remind them that God gives Mommies two arms and two "laps" (knees) for when both boys need help. A bit of double snuggling usually settles things enough so we can deal with problems sequentially. When one has an injury, however, I tell the other, "Brother has an emergency. Please help me for now, and I'll be with you as soon as this is solved."
Ann Hoffer, McLean, VA

In her ENCYCLOPEDIA A TO Z (Ballantine, $6.95), Ann Landers writes about two kinds of guilt, Earned and Unearned. Earned guilt, she says, comes when you do something "dishonest, hurtful, tacky, selfish or rotten." Spend two hours on it, then tell yourself, "Enough of this hair-shirt already."

There's another kind of guilt — the kind we lay on ourselves. Parents are especially susceptible to this kind. Judith Viorst, in LOVE & GUILT & THE MEANING OF LIFE, ETC. (Simon and Schuster, $5.95), gives a nice example:

"It is all right to leave your sick child with a sitter to go to a PTA meeting or to a save-the-whales meeting or to the drugstore to buy a heating pad. It is not all right to leave your sick child to go to a movie or out to lunch with friends or to the drugstore to buy eyeliner."

Every guilt on the list below has been admitted to by a living, breathing parent. Draw your own conclusions!

• Working away from home.
• Not working away from home.
• Being too strict.
• Not being strict enough.
• Expecting too much from children.
• Not expecting enough.
• Following the "experts'" advice when you know YOU'RE right.
• Not reading enough parenting books and articles.
• Having an only child.
• Having too many children.
• Not "playing" with the children, though you spend whole days with them.
• Playing with them so much that you don't have time for your housework or yourself.
• Being so immersed in child-centered volunteer activities that you don't have time to do things alone with your own kids.
• Feeling ashamed of a child for one reason or another.
• Yelling at the kids, when you're really mad at your spouse.
• Preparing to participate fully in your child's birth and then having to take an anesthetic or have a C-section.
• Doing everything the natural way, but having the baby in the hospital instead of at home.
• Depriving a child of a divorced spouse's live-in company and guidance.
• NOT FEELING GUILTY AT ALL, as far as the kids are concerned. (!)

parents forum

Q Were you disappointed with your child's gender?

We stupidly called the fetus "he" for nine months. I cried when my daughter was born and then felt guilty. When the second one came along I felt unhappy again and then relaxed and realized how many nice dresses she would get from her big sister.
Penny Dash   Cypress, CA

I wanted a boy, so I didn't dress up my girl until she was older. I think this was a benefit because she learned to crawl unencumbered by dresses, and she has a very self-confident attitude. After having a boy, I now wish I had two girls!
Kris Gialdini   Fremont, CA

We both wanted a girl. My husband wanted one because he is handicapped and felt it would be impossible for him to participate in those activities that a father is expected to share with his son (baseball, basketball, etc.). Well, last year our little girl played on a T-ball team. Just goes to show you!
Michele Olson   Blaine, MN

When I found out I was having a boy, I was glad. But I felt a moment of regret for the girl I was not going to have.
Unsigned

I'm thankful we had a girl first. My rancher husband is rather macho, and he wants our daughter to be "tough." But I know he is much more lenient and affectionate with her than he would have been with a boy. I think if our next one is a boy, my husband will be likely to have the same loving relationship with him that he now has with our daughter.
Mary Salsbury   Whitehall, MT

I have two boys now and I'd be just as happy if my third was another boy. There are advantages to both boys and girls and I was happy just to have healthy babies.
Christy Schmidt   Kerkhoven, MN

After two sons, I wanted a girl. About an hour before my third child was born, the nurse left me for a few minutes to assist with another delivery. When she came back I asked what that mother had had. The nurse said, "She had another boy and when we placed him in her arms she said, 'But I didn't want a boy.'" At that moment, I knew that I could never be disappointed with my baby as that mother was. When my son was born, I looked at his little face and knew I was in love again.
Jill Heasley   Fresno, CA

I wasn't disappointed with my first, but I wanted a girl the second time and I had another boy. So I have grieved. I resent comments about how I should be happy that he's healthy. Of course I am, but that doesn't take away my sadness and longing for a girl. We may adopt an older girl in the future.
Michele McBrayer   Georgetown, KY

We were both delighted with our daughter. It's interesting that since she is almost bald (at 9 mos.) there is less of a tendency to parent her differently from a boy. My husband especially has not been afraid to be rough in his play with her. Time will tell if this will change when her hair grows and she starts looking more like a girl.
Meg Saul   Cincinnati, OH

I'm sort of secretly (selfishly?) glad I have a daughter because the only way she'll ever know *exactly* how much I love her is when she has a baby of her own. I know (hope!) one day this will make us friends the way it has with my own mother.
Michele Price   Alexandria, VA

I have four daughters and I wasn't disappointed. You get whoever was in there. The lucky kids are delivered to parents who honestly don't care what sex they are.
Jackie Haag   Holden, MA

YES. Though my husband says he didn't care, I wanted a boy first (so did my mother-in-law). However, after our daughter's birth, I reasoned that having a little girl first would steer our family into a more loving, family-oriented, thoughtful unit. Also a little girl would be inclined to be helpful with a sibling in the future. Now that we have a girl, I wonder and worry how I will handle my disappointment if our next child is not a boy. (I might add that I would be equally desperate for a daughter if I'd had a boy first.)
Alice Bocknek   Burke, VA

I'm ashamed to admit it, but I prefer boys. I remember the way I treated *my* mother, and I don't want to have to go through that myself.
Fran Kane   Oakland, CA

Wrong-Gender-Baby Blues

Having expectations as to the sex of one's unborn child is a natural part of pregnancy. As evidence, consider all of the folk methods for determining a child's sex in utero.

Speculation regarding the gender of the unborn child is, in fact, beneficial. It encourages parents to think of their unborn offspring as a real person.

Parents who already have one or more children of one sex and none of the other sometimes experience feelings that are stronger than anticipation or expectation.

Parents unprepared for having a child of the opposite sex from what they had hoped for experience a variety of emotions after birth: disappointment, resentment, guilt for feeling the former, and failure. It is important to resolve these feelings as quickly as possible.

Otherwise, they can lead to overprotection when the prevailing emotion is guilt, or neglect when the feeling of resentment remains strong.

Virtually all professionals in the areas of family counselling and obstetrics agree that severe problems developing from unfulfilled child-gender expectations are rare.

One new potential source for stirring up the problem has arisen. Several theories have been circulating which claim to increase the chances of having a child of a pre-determined sex. A number of books explaining these theories are available.

Keep in mind theories claiming to increase the chances of having a boy as opposed to a girl or vice versa, alter the odds only slightly if at all.

Portland Family Calendar May, 1983

parents forum parent

Q What birth control method

The majority of the answers we received were in favor of sterilizing as the final choice once the preferred family size had been reached. Tubal ligation and vasectomy were favored about equally. Most readers who had already achieved this solution expressed a sense of relief at not having to worry about an "accident," a renewed spontaneity in their sex lives—and few doubts or regrets. We have chosen to publish answers which range over a variety of options and concerns.

Right now we are using condoms. I had been the one with the birth control responsibility for *years*, and now it's his turn. He plans to have a vasectomy soon.

Linda Chapman   Ft. Lauderdale, FL

When I am sure that I do not want any more children, I will consider getting my tubes tied. I have read a lot on the physical effects (good and bad), but have not read any informative articles about the psychological effects of tubal ligation.

Carol Caulk   Parkville, MD

After years of infertility, then two pregnancies back-to-back, we are suddenly faced with needing birth control. You have no idea how difficult it is to think about it at all after *years* of trying to conceive. We are using the pill now and trying to ease toward a permanent solution. Unfortunately we're at a stalemate—I feel like I've gone through enough already, and my husband is terrified of a vasectomy!

Pat Spiker   Columbus, OH

We are currently using the Billings Method (monitoring cervical mucus). This is an effective, non-invasive, natural method and I see no reason to change. I was sceptical at first, but we've used Billings successfully for more than three years.

Fran Kane   Oakland, CA

Last year my husband and I took a course and began using the sympto-thermal method of natural family planning (no, it is *not* rhythm). I had been using an IUD. It is fascinating to me, completely natural, and I am learning so much about the way my body works that I didn't know before. I'm satisfied, and not pregnant.

Harriet Landry   Belford, NJ

YES, I plan to change my method of birth control. I am now expecting our fourth child. We though we'd like to stop at two. . . then at three. Obviously, we were very "hit-and-miss" with our birth control. I plan to have a tubal ligation while I'm still in the hospital with this fourth (and *last*) child.

Elaine Gavin   Naperville, IL

I signed the consent forms for my tubal ligation while I was in the labor room after my third child. This was a very poor time to make this decision; right after labor you sure don't want another baby. We wish very badly we had waited for a few months for this decision. We have even considered a tubal reverse, but it's major surgery, expensive, and there's no guarantee it will work.

Jan Rhoades   Bowie, TX

We'll change to something permanent, but haven't decided which one of us yet.

Allyn Wiechert   O'Fallon, IL

My husband had a vasectomy four months after our third child was born and it was the *best* thing that happened in our early marriage. It was inexpensive, safe, not much discomfort, and fabulous for our sex lives!

Nedra O'Neill   Evergreen Park, IL

Consider The Options & Ratings

Here is the latest data on the newest. . . and oldest contraceptive techniques:

- *Sterilization* (male or female). It's the most popular form of birth control in the U.S. *Drawback:* Depending on the procedure used, reversal ranges from difficult to impossible. *Cost:* $1,180 for tubal ligation, $241 for vasectomy. *Pregnancy rate:* (per 100 couples in one year) Less than one.

- *Oral contraceptives.* The newest birth control pill releases different levels of hormones to accommodate different stages in a woman's reproductive cycle. It seems to reduce the frequency of ovarian, breast, and uterine tumors and pelvic inflammatory disease. It can lead to depression, weight gain, and cardiovascular problems in women who smoke, but this occurs rarely. *Average cost per year:* $172, including the cost of a visit to the doctor. *Pregnancy rate: 2-4.*

- *Condoms.* They are the best current protection against sexually transmitted disease, but can tear, leak, or slip off during intercourse. *Average cost per year:* $30. *Pregnancy rate: 10.*

- *Intrauterine devices (IUD).* An effective form of birth control, but can cause cramping and infection. Not recommended for women who have never been pregnant or who have many sex partners. *Average cost per year:* $131, including the visit to the physician for insertion. *Pregnancy rate: 5.*

- *Diaphragm.* Helps combat sexually transmitted diseases, and must be used with a spermicide to be effective. *Average cost per year:* $70. *Pregnancy rate: 15.9.*

- *Spermicide.* Protects but does not safeguard against venereal disease. For maximum protection against pregnancy, follow instructions precisely. *Average cost per year:* $50. *Pregnancy rate: 18.*

- *Contraceptive Sponge.* As good as spermicides at preventing VD. *Average cost per year:* $150. *Pregnancy rate: 9-15.*

- *Withdrawal.* Popular but highly unpredictable. *Average cost per year:* $0. *Pregnancy rate: 23.*

- *Natural family planning.* Various systems are used to determine a woman's fertile period. The couple abstains from sex during that time. *Average cost per year:* $0. *Pregnancy rate: 24.*

- *Cervical cap.* Never achieved wide acceptance due to difficulty of insertion and removal. Not yet approved for general use in the U.S. *Drawback:* Level of effectiveness has not been documented yet. Presently available in only a few sizes. *Average cost per year:* $100.

forum parents forum

do you and your spouse use?

I got pregnant the first time while on the pill, and the second time while using the condom/foam combination. So we switched to Natural Family Planning (observing mucus/temperature changes) and have not conceived in five years. As an added bonus, because you have to abstain during the middle of your cycle, it has really perked up our sex life—you know you always want it more when you can't have it!

Unsigned

We decided that I would have a tubal ligation done about six months after our second (and last) child was born. It's been more than three years now, and I just can't bring myself to schedule the operation, however minor it may be. My husband has not volunteered to have a vasectomy, so we are coasting along with the rhythm method. I'm 42 now and hoping for an early menopause.

Unsigned

I keep considering a tubal ligation, but I'm not too convinced that I don't want any more kids. It varies with the kind of day I'm having. Plus the Catholic Church is *so* opposed to it.

Kathryn Richardson   Fort Defiance, AZ

We chose a vasectomy. It is less traumatic than a tubal ligation, and cheaper in money and time lost. We're very pleased with it.

Unsigned

I had problems with cysts while on the pill, and found diaphragms and jelly/foam to be messy and disruptive. I didn't like the IUD because it can abort a fertilized egg, so I had my tubes tied four years ago, and have medical problems ever since. Also, I always feel depressed after seeing a new baby— even though I *thought* I didn't want any more. I wish I had found a better answer.

Peg Murphy   S. Suburban, IL

The Sure-Fire Conception Plan for Your Second Child

- *Buy an expensive two-bedroom house*
- *Sell all your baby furniture at a garage sale*
- *Buy a new post-pregnancy wardrobe*
- *Finally train your first child to sleep through the night*

If your parents were unable to have children, you won't be able to have children either.

(Meadowbrook; $2.95)
Excerpt from Mother Murphy's Law

I am 36, have four children and plan no more. I know its time to do something premanent, but there is a part of me that is unwilling to admit my childbearing years and girlhood are behind me.

Unsigned

My husband plans to have a vasectomy. This was totally his idea, and I'm proud that he is secure enough to choose what is obviously the simplest solution.

Brigid Brooks   Forest Park, IL

After my second C-section (at 33) I had my tubes cut and tied while still on the operating table. I have mixed feelings about having had this done. Many times I would have gone ahead and gotten pregnant for the third time (like every time I saw or held an infant), and then I probably would have hated myself afterward. Neither of my first two pregnancies was easy or comfortable, we really can't afford a third child, and my aging body couldn't easily handle another C-section. So, although I have intermittent regrets, it was probably the smart thing to do!

Jamee McGaughan   Bear, DE

I may have my tubes tied. But it's a scary, permanent move, and I keep hearing about previously unknown, long-term side effects, so no decision is made yet. No rush, I guess.

Lenie Bershad   Southfield, MI

We have three children, one of whom was planned. My husband recently had a vasectomy, and yes, we're happy with our choice.

Denise Voeller   Coon Rapids, MN

After this child (our third) is born, I will have a tubal ligation. I already feel good about this decision. We love kids, but three is our limit.

Vicki Piippo   Richland, WA

I have used the Copper 7 IUD for eight years and am using it between children and will use it after the last. We will probably opt for a vasectomy for my husband when we reach our mid-forties.

Patti O'Connell   Dallas, TX

Methods in the Making

- An *agar gel* diaphragm that protects against conception and then liquifies within several hours.
- Hormone-releasing vaginal rings that protect against conception.
- Hormone injections that prevent ovulation for three to six months.
- A penile cap made from contraceptive film. These caps cover the head of the penis only, and are made of very thick film that is washed off after use. It's in early stages of development.
- An under the skin implant for women that works like an oral contraceptive. *Bonus:* a single implant prevents pregnancy for five years. One type is already being used in several countries, and a second version is being tested for use in the U.S.
- Research on a male oral contraceptive has been disappointing. Injecting a man with a synthetic version of the hormone that controls sperm production seems to reduce but not stop it, and has caused temporary impotence.

Privileged Information   January, 1986

parents forum paren

Q How do you and your spouse divide household and child-rearing chores?

Ha ha—ho ho—hee hee. I think I was born 20 years too soon, but he's such a great human, and we're both happy with things undivided. We have our own space this way.
Merrie Ann Handley, Boulder Creek, CA

We have a two-level house. Chores are listed on a chart. We alternate floors each week. My husband does weekend meals, puts our older boy to bed each night and takes major childcare responsibility on weekends.
Elaine Whitlock, Northampton, MA

He does all the work he possibly can and so do I. We don't make lists and keep count on who's going to punish whom and how. If one of us feels overwhelmed, we talk.
Unsigned, Marina Del Ray, CA

When my job was being a banker, I would have been surprised and insulted if my husband showed up to help with household chores. The same applies now. I am extremely proud of my job and the way I do it.
Kathy Hickok, Delray Beach, FL

My husband was reared in a family of five boys and six girls. The boys never lifted a finger; the girls waited on them hand and foot. When we were first married he would tap his glass with his fork when he wanted more milk! Things changed fast around here. Now, six-and-a half years and two kids later, he does his fair share about 75 percent of the time, and he puts in 10- to 12-hour days at work. This year he's not going to play softball and we'll be able to take the kids biking and swimming more often.
Jeanne Gretter, Sigourney, IA

We realized from the day Jennie was born that I was staying home during the day to be with her, not to clean house. I recommend HOW TO BE A MOTHER AND A PERSON, TOO, by Shirley Radl (Rawson, Wade, $7.95)—it deals very practically with this question. And here's a perfect quote from a grandmother: "God did give mothers two pairs of hands. The other pair is on the father's arms."
Ella Beth Goetschius, Houston, TX

Very easily—50/50. I do my half, and then I do his half!
Peggy Nelson, Deephaven, MN

My husband started vacuuming and cleaning the bathroom while I was pregnant and has continued to do so. This takes enough away from me that I'm satisfied. As to child care, a friend told me to "make" him help from the first day; don't let him get lazy; get him to help while the baby is new and it's fun. It works. He's used to diapers, feeding, all of it. None of the baby care is a chore—it's a way of life.
Margie Goodell, Toledo, OH

When my husband is home he bathes at least one child and puts them both to bed with a story. He does absolutely no cleaning, cooking or washing. He will iron his own shirts, since I don't do them well enough.
Unsigned, Atlantic City, NJ

Come on, now. Housework is not the most difficult of occupations. My husband and I both work full time. We spend no more than 11 hours a week on housework, including cooking. Sometimes our house is a little untidy, but we cover the basics, enjoy our careers and put time with our daughter as a top priority.

I think caring for young children is one thing, housework another. It bothers me to see them confused. It also bothers me to see how defensive full-time homemakers are. No one has a right to question a woman or a man about the decision to care for children full time, but housework is a full-time job only when you make it that way.
Ginnie Nuta, Gaithersburg, MD

Guests "freak out" at the casual way my husband handles bathing our girls, 1 and 3. They all think I have him "trained." Actually, he enjoys child care and does as much as he can to help, at least 50/50 when he's home.
Belinda Stanley, Sugar Land, TX

I had a big mouth before I had kids. I said I couldn't see why anyone who stayed home all day couldn't do all the housework—so I do most of it. But my husband is perfectly willing to help in a pinch, or if I ask him.
Vicky Lauritzen, Fall River, WI

We both have full-time, demanding jobs. Each of us takes responsibility for getting one child ready in the morning and getting the other ready for bed at night. That way we have quality time exposure to each child. Playtime activity is done as a family. One of us cooks dinner, the other cleans up. Major household duties get left to the once-a-week housekeeper—the best investment yet!
Karen Bergher, Anaheim, CA

HERE'S HOW!

In his book IS THERE LIFE AFTER HOUSEWORK (Writer's Digest Books), Don Aslett tells everything one could want to know about getting and keeping a clean, well-organized house. And the answer to the question is YES, he says, in 17 chapters on everything from cleaning furniture, walls, ceilings, floors and windows to getting rid of junk to learning the truth about old wives' tales. On the subject of sharing chores he offers two tips:

• Refuse to be the janitor for the kids' and husband's messes. Picking up after them is bad for everyone involved. You teach irresponsiblity perfectly by assuming responsibility for someone else, except those who don't know any better or can't help themselves. Insist that everyone clean up his or her own messes and premises. Don't send husband to work or children to school undisciplined.

• Write down and post needs. When you demand or ask for help, many family members will begin to assist you. Written messages eliminate short memories and the innocent phrase, "I didn't know you needed anything done."

forum parents forum

My husband is a doctor, working sometimes 100 hours a week, so he doesn't have time to help out much, and I don't expect him to. He will care for our daughter when I ask him to. In this situation it's almost mandatory for someone to stay home full time and hold our home together. I resent all the articles about husband and wife sharing house and child care equally. For us it's impossible. I'm just lucky I don't have to work as hard as he does.

Mrs. L. Peters, San Antonio, TX

My husband and I both work outside the home and have no cut and dried assignments. When the clothes are climbing out of the hamper or the dishes are fermenting in the sink, he gets the message and chips in. He likes to cook almost as much as I do, so some nights when I get home dinner is ready—DELIGHTFUL! He's a devoted father; these chores just come naturally to him.

Evelyn Wasniewski, New Egypt, NJ

We consider ourselves "even" when my husband is home evenings and weekends. Then, tasks are divided by interest and ability: I cook, he does mending, etc. Some things we do together, such as bed-changing.

Susan Merl, Walnut Creek, CA

Since in our society my earning potential is less than half that of my husband, he works at business and I work at home.

SallyAnn Winterle, St. Pual, MN

Very conventionally. Since I'm home all day with the children, the everyday drudgery is pretty much left to me. The home upkeep and repair drudgery is left to my husband. We share equally the JOYS of child rearing.

Jenny Schroeder, LaCrosse, WI

We don't divide; I do all but carry out the garbage. But I married a farmer who has his own 12- to 16-hour days. I find him very adept at after-supper chores with the four kids when I abandon him to go to aerobic class two evenings a week.

Debbie Megginson, Auburn, IL

I used to do almost everything myself until my husband was laid off from his job and realized how hard I work and how the children wear me down. Now he pitches in and takes over quite a bit, and I just get out of the way and let him go.

Joyce Rospiler, Industry, PA

Before we were married, my husband and I agreed that we were equal partners. Unfortunately, his idea of how much there is to do is different from mine. He thinks the yard needs mowing when the city threatens to cut it, floors and bathroom should be cleaned when someone's coming over, dishes should be done when none are clean. Therefore, I do it all, because I can't stand things that dirty.

Unsigned

Some People Suffer In Silence Louder Than Others

Have you ever heard as you lie comatose on your pillow at night, a line like this? "Say darling, how come you never get the ring out of the bathtub?" If you have, you might feel, as Carol Eisen described in NOBODY SAID YOU HAD TO EAT OFF THE FLOOR (a book now out of print, but available in some libraries):

• I spent the whole day cleaning out the rotten closets, including *his* rotten closet, and he doesn't even mention it. (Hostility.)

• Why can't he clean out the bloody ring in the tub if he cares so much about it? He never helps me anyway. (Hostility.)

• I'm a lousy wife. (Depression.)
• I *should* keep the bathtub clean. (Guilt.)
And your husband might feel:

• I worked hard all day. Is it too much to expect a clean bathtub which my mother always had? (Hostility.)

• Why the devil is she so tired? So big deal, she cleaned out my closet and now I'll never be able to find anything. (Hostility.)

• If I were better at what I did I could afford to get her a maid and we wouldn't have these problems. (Guilt.)

• I'm rotten. (Guilt.)

It's remarkable, says the author, how many fights get started this way.

Q How do you disagree when children are present?

I blow my top and later am terribly remorseful because my 3-year-old was watching. I am determined that I've done that for the last time and so far have been successful. Praying does wonders to calm me down.

Vicky Saliba, Edmond, OK

We continue our disagreements in front of the kids unless they are too time-consuming (then the kids get impatient!). My parents never argued in front of me, and when my husband and I argued the first time, I thought it meant he didn't love me.

Shirley Cohn, Vancouver, B.C.

My husband and I usually handle a dis-agreement when it arises. Consequently, our daughter witnesses a few of them. We don't like to wait until late at night, when we're tired and edgy after a long day. Usually her response is, "Stop it, KIDS!", and with a smile she wraps her arms around us both. She senses discord, but I feel she is aware that it's part of life.

Kathy Lord, Rochester, MN

If the disagreement is quite serious, we wait until the children are asleep. The smaller squabbles are treated as a normal part of a relationship. If the older child wonders why Mom and Dad seem unhappy, I explain that, as he gets angry with his brother, We don't always see eye to eye. I explain also that it is not serious and that we still love each other.

Mrs. M. Kunc, Swartz Creek, MI

I think it's healthy for a child to see his parents disagree, provided the disagree-ments don't concern childrearing. My 4-year-old has disagreements galore with his friends and with us. I think it helps him accept this "disagreeable" side of himself and see that even grown-ups can't always get along together.

Pat Brinkmann, Palo Alto, CA

We handle disagreements between our-selves as we do those between us and the kids—we give each other a nice, strong "I" message (as in Parent Effectiveness Train-ing) and work from there. We are open and honest and basically disagree only about the housework anyway. Not only do we show that we have nothing to hide, our kids are modeling well on our example.

Cheryl Chapman, Brookfield, IL

We use a combination of methods. Since most of the disagreements are over dealing with our children, I find that biting my tongue and discussing things later works best. However, we often voice our different views on other subjects. It's a healthy example for our children to see their parents work things out and remain friendly. On the other hand, when one of us needs to "hash it out" then and there, we'll have them leave to play elsewhere or do a small favor. Children can also learn to appreciate their parents' need for privacy.

Jodi Junge, Huntingdon Valley, PA

Our 1-year-old tends to cry when our voices get too loud or angry. However, as he matures, I hope to teach him that it's healthy to express his feelings and that disagree-ments can be resolved through communica-tion. I think this is an especially important lesson for boys to learn.

Janet Stabile, Ellington, CT

We save it for when our son is asleep or not around. No sense upsetting him when it's not his problem.

W. Lyles, Aurora, CO

We don't "send" the kids to their rooms, we tell them to go "hide" in their rooms. They think it's a game. Sometimes, though, we talk it all out in front of them, but that's probably not too good, right?

Jill Heasley, Fresno, CA

Our 3-year-old is just beginning to realize that something is wrong when we argue. We try to keep things on a discussion basis in front of the kids and not let things escalate. I have admitted to the kids that I am mad at Daddy, but I always add, "But I still love him." Sometimes just saying this dissolves my anger.

Barbara Sattora, Rush, NY

When I was a child, my parents argued often, and almost always in front of us kids. I remember feeling very nervous and worried about the welfare of their marriage, so I've always been sensitive in this area. We try to keep the kids out of our disagreements, but we find it to be impossible all the time. When we notice that the kids are nervous, we take a moment out, each take a child, give big hugs and kisses, and explain to them that even if we don't agree about everything we still love each other AND them very much. When the yelling and screaming are over and the problem resolved, we all participate in the make-up hugs and kisses.

Valerie Cook, SugarLand, TX

We let them in on it. Once during a very vocal disagreement I broke two plates, leav-ing a hole in the vinyl flooring. We bought a rug to cover it, and on occasion our 4-year-old used to proudly throw back the rug to show our indiscretions to his amigos (and ours!).

Kathy Hickok, Delray Beach, FL

Letting Off Steam

A lot has been written about how spouses can argue "constructively," but little is avail-able on handling arguments when children are present. There are some things you shouldn't argue about at all in front of them, say the experts. Some of these are money, child-rearing policies in general (though an occasional disagreement about a specific matter isn't harmful), your relatives, per-sonal sex matters and, of course, the chil-dren themselves. It's not considered harmful to argue about some other things in front of the kids—in fact, it will help them realize you're human—but there are some guide-lines that are helpful.

• Let the children observe occasional disagreements about everyday matters, and let them see you settle them in a reasonable, mature way.

• Be sure the kids know that an argument has ended, that the issue has been resolved. Let them see you make up or apologize and let them know you still love each other (and them!).

• Don't force a child to be responsible for your actions by letting him or her assume the role of peacemaker or choose sides.

• Try to avoid verbal abuse when you argue—it can be frightening, and it's a habit you don't want the kids to imitate. And ALWAYS avoid physical violence.

• Don't argue about anything so often that your kids will grow up remembering you as always angry with each other.

> ONE OF THE WORST FEELINGS IS WHEN YOU GET HALFWAY THROUGH AN ARGUMENT WITH YOUR SPOUSE AND SUDDENLY REALIZE THAT HE OR SHE IS RIGHT.

parentsforum

Q How do you settle parenting differences?

Some fathers have a difficult time showing emotions for their children. The only way they know how to show it is by wrestling and teasing. This contact is good for the children, but it will drive every mother and wife out of her mind!

Dolores DalSanto   Florence, WI

Usually, I'll make a face or sigh and he'll get the message and stop. Then, later, he'll ask me what I felt he was doing wrong.

Janet Bauer   Islip Terrace, NY

He doesn't really tease, but unappreciated behavior is discussed as unhealthy psychological experiences for·a much too impressionable developing personality.

P. Woods   Ridgewood, NJ

He doesn't tease in a hurtful way, so it hasn't been a problem. If I felt strongly that he was doing something hurtful to our son, I would discuss it with him—but he loves our son as much as I do, and the two of them need to find their own relationship without my interference, so I'd have to feel really strongly about the issue.

Lisa Mead Hughes   Santa Clara, CA

I tend to read him quotes from child-development books that do not support his actions.

Margaret Fisher Cutter   NE, PA

Views expressed by husbands are not necessarily those of the management.

I just tell my husband I don't like what he is saying or teaching Sara and usually we discuss the remark. Usually all I have to say is "Do you want your daughter saying that?" and that is the end of the discussion. But we all say things that we regret and mothers are by no means exempt. My daughter did something silly the other day and I said "What a dummy" regretting it the second the words were out of my mouth. Well, you can guess what Sara's word for the day was!

Karen Drotzer   Corton-on-Hudson, NY

We usually talk about the feeling and compromise. Fortunately, my husband is very understanding on these matters. He sees a woman as the one who sets the guidelines for the children.

Linda Kaye Wiesman   Elizabethtown, PA

I don't handle my husband's teasing well at all. I usually yell at him which makes him do it all the more. Unfortunately the kids hear my disapproval and side with me, much to my husband's dismay. I've tried discussing this with him privately, but his idea of teasing and mine are definitely not the same!

Maryanne Shutan   Highland Park, IL

Trust your wife's judgment—look at who she married!

Nag, nag, nag—I bug my hsuband during his favorite shows on TV.

Pam Stuart   Tulsa, OK

I tell him right away. If my daughter doesn't like it, she repeats what I say. If she likes it, she tells me, "It's all right Mommy." (He tickles her.)

Carol Caulk   Parkville, MO

I advise him to set his limits by the child's response. For example, a few seconds of tickling produces a giggle. More than that produces tears. Obviously, tickling to the point of tears is not healthy for children. Husbands sometimes need to be told what is good for kids, especially if they can't spend much time with them and don't know them as well as the full-time caretaker.

Brynne Garman   Kent, WA

When my husband gives a punishment or makes a statement I don't agree with I make him back it up. If my son complains I tell him it is between him and his dad. Sometimes my husband sees it through, sometimes he gives a little because then he knows I disagree, and sometimes he forgets to carry out his harsh decree.

Claudine Mitchell   Peculiar, MO

The only thing I don't like that my husband does is watch certain movies that worry me (i.e., *King Kong, Frankenstein, Star Wars*). We only allow 30 minutes of TV a night, but my son cherishes these half hour movie breaks with his father.

Stephanie Clagnaz   East Meadow, NY

I tell him immediately and assertively. This usually elicits a defensive response, but is very effective. The children remember and won't let him get away with it again. He does the same thing to me.

Cheryl Kronberger   Oak Park, MI

I softly say something like, "Honey, don't you think he's had enough tickling?" That usually makes him aware of what he's doing, rather than being carried away with the excitement/behavior.

Donna Theilen   Waukegan, IL

I really object to having the radio blasting in a car, or a TV in a home when children are trying to talk, or do homework, or just want to be family. It really bothers me when we parents treat children as if they are an interference to our listening or viewing pleasures and then we turn around and jump all over them for not listening!

Nedra O'Neill   Evergreen Park, IL

My husband is entitled to his theories too, so if what he does with the kids bothers me I try to leave the room and get involved in something else. Then I remind myself that he represents the male image and I can't do that. I'm responsible for being their mother, not father too!

Jill Heasley   Freson, CA

My husband constantly picks on our oldest son (9½), and puts him down. I have tried talking to my husband (which doesn't work), standing up for my son, protesting, etc. Nothing works. If I felt I could support myself and three kids, I'd leave. I talk to my son and try to help him understand.

Unsigned

If I didn't understand you so well, I wouldn't disagree with you so much.

Ashley Brillant

My theory is that I can't change people. I pointed out to the offender that the relationship he is building is the foundation for a relationship that will continue through his life. My dad didn't communicate on a meaningful level with me when I was growing up, and when he grew old, I did not communicate with him. I make sure that I always try to be the best I can with the kids so my future friendship with them will be good.

Karen Haynes   Upper Marlboro, MD

the PRACTICAL PARENTING BOOKSHELF

Collect this excellent library of parenting books on important topics for parents.
Buy the 6 book collection for the special price of $16.95 (reg $22.75). **[#B.Set, $16.95]**

TOILET TRAINING
Helpful advice explaining readiness plus practical hints for daytime and nighttime training. Product information and resources.
[#B.TT] $3.95

WELCOMING YOUR SECOND BABY
Help your child prepare for the new baby and promote good self-esteem. Tips cover your hospital stay to dealing with jealousy and regression.
[#B.2B] $3.95

GETTING YOUR BABY TO SLEEP-AND BACK TO SLEEP
Practical tips to deal with babies who don't sleep-like babies plus ideas for waking toddlers, and help with naps and nightmares.
[#B.SL] $3.95

TRAVELING WITH YOUR BABY
Ideas for car, plane and train travel—home and abroad. Covers planning ahead, eating and sleeping away from home.
[#B.TR] $2.95

BIRTHDAY PARTIES
Best ideas to organize easy and successful parties for the first eight years! Decorations, games, food ideas plus age-related considerations.
[#B.BP] $3.95

DEAR BABYSITTER HANDBOOK
This guide taken from *Dear Babysitter* (below) provides a less expensive guide for your sitter. A medical release form and the needed fill-in-facts forms.
[#B.DB] #3.95

...by parents...   ...for parents...

PRACTICAL PARENTING TIPS FOR THE FIRST FIVE YEARS
The best "it worked for me" ideas from diapering to getting kids ready for preschool.
[#P1] $6.95 spiral

BEST OF *VICKI LANSKY'S* PRACTICAL PARENTING NEWSLETTER
A wonderful collection of parents' responses on major issues: the big issues(like discipline), the philosophical issues; the nuts-and-bolts issues, the husband-wife issues and the *guilt* issues. From its 9 years of national publication! 8x11" format. **[#P3] $5.95**

PRACTICAL PARENTING FOR THE SCHOOL-AGE YEARS
Excellent advice and tips for living with 6-12 yr olds. Covers homework, hobbies, allowances, setting limits and more. **[#P2] $5.95**

DEAR BABYSITTER HANDBOOK/NOTEPAD
Everything your sitter needs to know... in one place in easy-to-use hardcover book. 48 page handbook with bedtime strategies, first-aid, a medical release form, and more, plus a 50 sheet tear-off pad.
[#DBS] $7.95

COMPLETE GUIDE TO PREGNANCY AND CHILD CARE
THE reference book to take you through pregnancy and child care. Illustrated. Tips from shopping for cribs to toys to doctors. Guide to common illnesses. 432 pages.
[#CG] $14.95 hardbound

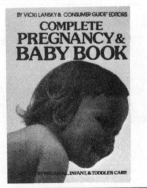

FEED YOUR KIDS RIGHT with...

OVER 1 MILLION COPIES SOLD!

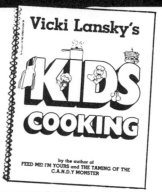

FEED ME I'M YOURS
Best selling baby food, toddler food cookbook. Over 200 child-tested recipes & practical feeding advice.
[#FM] $6.95 spiral
[#FMp] 3.50 paperback

TAMING OF THE CANDY MONSTER
Fabulous cookbook to help wean children on to betterfor-you snacks and meals. Brown bag ideas, microwave quickies, milk-free cooking plus good tips for shopping.
[#CM] $2.95 paperback

KIDS COOKING
Step-by-step recipes for kids 8-12 to make. In color: desserts, snacks, mini-meals & holiday fun. Spiral binding. [#KC] $5.95
(*not available until Sept '87*)

KOKO BEAR "*READ-TOGETHER*" BOOKS for parents and kids!

The most important way you can help your child understand *what to expect* and *what's expected* ...plus tips on every page for parents... Lovely, colored illusrations featuring KOKO BEAR, a unisex bear, who will delight and educate!

available Nov'87

KOKO BEAR'S NEW POTTY
KoKo learns how nice dry diapers can be by learning to use first a potty seat and then the toilet. KoKo is still loved even when an accident happens. KoKo's big bear pants and successes will delight you and your child. [#K.NP] $3.95

A NEW BABY AT KOKO BEAR'S HOUSE
MaMa and PaPa Bear share their exciting news—there's going to be a new baby bear! KoKo goes through the key stages of pregnancy, birth and MaMa's homecoming—and even a bit of jealously. [#K.NB] $3.95

KOKO BEAR'S NEW BABYSITTER
When KoKo's parents go out for the evening, KoKo is concerned about their leaving and the new sitter, but Penny Panda and KoKo have a wonderful evening.
[#K.BS] $3.95

KOKO BEAR BIG EAR ACHE
(*Preparing for Ear Tube Surgery*) KoKo's ear aches lead to the need for ear tubes at the hospital in a day surgical routine. Q & A section on common parental concerns.
[#K.EA] $3.95

BEST BUYS FOR PARENTS

DON'T LEAVE HOME WITHOUT IT!

LET YOUR BABY SLEEP LIKE ONE!

HELP YOUR CHILD ADJUST TO NEW BABY!

BABY FOOD GRINDER

TAKE-ALONG FOLD-UP POTTY SEAT ADAPTER This wonderful plastic adapter folds to a 5" square to fit in your purse. [#AD] $4.50

AUDIO TAPE: *GET YOUR BABY TO SLEEP* Author reads helpful sleep tips for new babies on side one; soothing lullabies with heatbeat sounds on side two will put your baby to sleep. It works! [#TP] $7.95

BIG BROTHER/BIG SISTER T-SHIRTS Promote self-esteem in older child. Short sleeve, all cotton t-shirts Indicate size:S(8)-M(10)-L(12).
[#T-B] blue $10.00
[#T-S] pink $10.00

BABY FOOD GRINDER
Make nutritious baby food yourself at home and away easily—with this plastic grinder. Acts as serving dish. Feeding spoon included. [#GR] $8.95

To order any of these books or buys, send check, money order, or Visa/MasterCard information (plus expiration date) to:

PRACTICAL PARENTING, 18326 Minnetonka Blvd, Deephaven, MN 55391

To charge an order, call 1-800-255-3379; for information, call (612) 475-3527.

ADD THE FOLLOWING POSTAGE TO ANY ORDER:
If your order totals under $5, add $1.50 for shipping and handling. For orders of $5-$10,...add $2; on $10-$20,...add $3; and on orders of $20 or more,...add $4.00.

Vicki Lansky's
practical parenting

18326 Minnetonka Blvd • Deephaven, MN 55391 • (612) 475-3527

TO ORDER,* CALL TOLL FREE 1-800-255-3379
Mon-Fri. 9am to 5pm, C.T.
Customer Service (612) 475-3527

ORDER FORM

Name _____

Address _____

City/St _____ zip _____

daytime phone ( ) _____

TO SEND MERCHANDISE TO ANOTHER ADDRESS:

item codes# _____

To: _____

address _____

city/st _____ zip _____

☐ Enclose card from: _____

---

*CHARGE TO MY ACCOUNT   ☐ VISA   ☐ MasterCard   Exp.Date _____

Acct# _____   Signature _____

billing address, if different: _____

Item code	Description of item	quantity	price	total
	Thank you for your order!			

Total for Merchandise		
In Mn, residents add 6% tax of above		
Shipping/handling (see chart)		
Additional $2 fee for UPS delivery		
TOTAL AMOUNT		

SHIPPING AND HANDLING:
If your order totals
up to $5.00 .... add $1.50
from $5.01 to $10 .... add $2.00
from $10.01 to $20 .... add $3.00
from $20.01 up .... add $4.00
Optional: add additional $2 for UPS delivery.

*Enclose check for this amount to **Practical Parenting**. (In Canada, US funds only.)*

tape edges if check is enclosed

Vicki Lansky's

practical parenting

**18326 Minnetonka Blvd
Deephaven, MN 55391**